COOKING WITH
TRADER Joe's
COOKBOOK

COMPANION

DEANA GUNN ❀ WONA MINIATI

Cooking with Trader Joe's – Companion
By Deana Gunn and Wona Miniati
Photographs by Deana Gunn & Wona Miniati
Designed by Lilla Hangay

Published by Brown Bag Publishers, LLC
P. O. Box 235065
Encinitas, CA 92023-5065
info@cookTJ.com

Printed in Singapore by Imago

Library of Congress Cataloging-in-Publication Data
Gunn, Deana & Miniati, Wona.
The Cooking with Trader Joe's Cookbook: Companion /
by Deana Gunn & Wona Miniati: 2nd ed.
Includes index.
I. Quick and easy cookery. 2 Trader Joe's (Store) I. Title.

ISBN 978-0-9799384-9-8

Table of Contents

Thank You Notes   4

About This Book   5

About Us   6

Nutritional Data   8

Useful Conversions   7

Appealing Appetizers   9

Soups & Salads   19

Main Meals   37

Simple Sides   99

Delicious Desserts & Daring Drinks   121

Breakfast Beginnings   151

Index   163

Trader Joe's Store Locations   175

Thank You Notes

Much love and thanks to our wonderful families, who supported us through this second book, while they cheered on the success of our first book.

We applaud Lilla Hangay, our talented designer, for exceptionally fun designs that make our books stand out from the crowd. We praise our editor, Larry Gunn, for thoughtfully and artfully improving our book every step of the way. We are grateful to nutritionist Eddy Kim for his thorough nutritional analysis of all our recipes.

Our gratitude and admiration goes out to Trader Joe's, which continues to provide us with the fuel for our passion and the excitement of new culinary finds. We like to think of ourselves as being among your biggest fans! A special thanks to our local Trader Joe's crew members, whose friendliness and helpfulness always make us feel right at home. You make Trader Joe's the fun shopping experience that it is.

And of course, our deepest thanks to our fans and readers, who truly made our independent cookbooks a grassroots success across the country. Your enthusiasm in spreading the word about our cookbooks has opened doors that would have otherwise been impossible to navigate. We've been delighted to interact with you via our website, blog, book signings, and other events. It's always a treat to hear about your favorite products and your own Trader Joe's recipes.

Our heartfelt thanks to you all!

About This Book

When we wrote our first cookbook, "Cooking with All Things Trader Joe's," we had no idea it would become such a runaway hit with Trader Joe's fans across the country. We heard from enthusiastic moms, students, men, women, singles, families, retirees, and busy professionals. In addition to their love of Trader Joe's, they had something else in common. They loved good food but didn't want to (or couldn't) spend all day in the kitchen making it. Within the pages of our cookbook, they discovered easy and accessible recipes, delicious meals, and new favorite products at Trader Joe's.

We heard from people who carried their cookbooks into Trader Joe's stores in order to plan and shop for meals, and from people who even kept an extra copy in their car! We thought it would be great to create a handy cookbook in a convenient size. This collection of recipes includes favorite recipes from our first cookbook, favorite recipes from our popular blog, and some recipes that are being unveiled here for the first time. In this revised edition, we added nutritional data, gluten-free index, vegetarian index, and photos.

As before, capitalized ingredients in this book refer to a specific Trader Joe's product. Some ingredients are seasonal, and occasionally there is a product that is discontinued. For these scenarios, we always try to suggest a few substitutions and alternatives within the recipes. We offer a "substitutions" section on our website (www.cookTJ.com) where we keep an updated, real-time list of substitutions for any Trader Joe's ingredients that have gone the way of the passenger pigeon.

About Us

We're not Trader Joe's employees or affiliated with the store. We're two very devoted Trader Joe's fans who decided to share our recipes and time-saving tips with fellow fans like you. We developed our recipes over the last 14 years of shopping at Trader Joe's, exploring their amazing assortment of affordable gourmet products, and making food that we loved.

Over the years, we found ourselves growing increasingly busier, first with a career and then with young kids. We no longer had time to cook meals from scratch, the way our mothers had taught us. We started using little shortcuts, whether it was ready-made pizza dough, curry sauce, jarred bruschetta, or pre-cut vegetables. With shortcuts like these, our preparation times went from an hour (or more) to less than 15 minutes. We could create healthy, homemade meals, any night of the week, in a snap.

The way we cook is similar to how a restaurant chef or a TV chef creates meals almost magically in a matter of 10-15 minutes. How do they do that? It's only possible because the prep crew has come in earlier in the day to wash and chop vegetables, create sauces, start pastries, and marinate meats. We started thinking of Trader Joe's as our prep crew. We'd be the chefs who took advantage of the time-consuming, laborious work behind the scenes, and we'd create delicious meals almost effortlessly.

Useful Conversions

Volume Measurements:

3 teaspoons = 1 tablespoon

4 tablespoons = ¼ cup

16 tablespoons = 1 cup

2 cups = 1 pint

2 pints = 1 quart

4 quarts = 1 gallon

2 tablespoons = 1 fluid ounce

1 cup = 8 fluid ounces

Weight Measurements:

16 ounces = 1 pound

Abbreviations:

tsp = teaspoon

Tbsp = tablespoon

oz = ounce

lb = pound

pkg = package

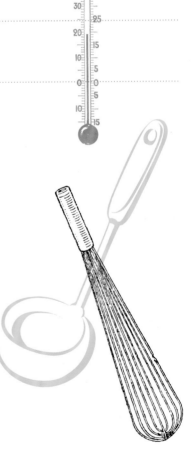

Nutritional Data

Each recipe has been analyzed by a certified nutritionist for nutritional content. Optional ingredients are not included when calculating nutritional data. Serving sizes follow FDA guidelines and dietitian recommendations.

Each recipe contains indicators for recipes that are

gluten-free   **vegetarian**

Please note that the FDA does not yet regulate gluten-free labeling. Products at Trader Joe's may be labeled "no gluten ingredients used" which does not necessarily exclude the chance of cross-contamination if they are produced in a facility that handles gluten products. Persons with celiac disease or severe gluten allergies should note that unless a product is labeled and tested gluten-free by standards such as ELISA and produced in a dedicated facility, there is possibility of cross-contamination.

Appealing Appetizers

Homemade Hummus

Hummus is a thick and smooth spread made of mashed garbanzo beans (also called chickpeas or ceci beans), olive oil, lemon juice, garlic, and tahini – very popular across the world. It's a breeze to pick it up ready-made, but it's almost as easy to make your own, As with many things, the one you make fresh at home is often the best! A few hours or even a day in the fridge gives the flavors time to meld and makes it even more delicious.

2 (15-oz) cans garbanzo beans

1 clove garlic, crushed, or 1 cube frozen Crushed Garlic

½ tsp cumin

¼ tsp salt

1 Tbsp sesame tahini

¼ cup extra virgin olive oil

2 Tbsp lemon juice (juice of 1 lemon)

1 Drain one of the cans of beans. Add both cans (including the juices of one can) to blender or food processor.

2 Add remaining ingredients and purée until hummus is smooth.

3 For best flavor, store in fridge for a few hours before serving.

Tip: When serving, garnish with pine nuts, a sprinkle of paprika, a drizzle of olive oil, or chopped parsley. Serve with pita chips, pita bread, vegetables, or in a wrap or falafel sandwich.

Prep time: *10 minutes,* Serves *10*

Per serving: 124 calories, 6 g fat, 1 g saturated fat, 4 g protein, 14 g carbs, 4 g fiber, 1 g sugar, 339 mg sodium

Tomato and Mozzarella Skewers

Stick it to Caprese with this cute appetizer, which has all the classic flavors of Italy on a little stick. If you liked the Caprese Salad in our original cookbook, Cooking with All Things Trader Joe's, you'll love this party-ready version. We've combined the traditional pairings of tomatoes, mozzarella, and basil into an easy and festive appetizer with all the colors of red, white, and *skew*. Who says finger food can't be classy?

1 (8-oz) container Ciliegine fresh mozzarella balls

1 (8-oz) pkg cherry tomatoes or grape tomatoes

1 bunch fresh basil leaves

1 Tbsp olive oil

Pinch salt

Pinch black pepper

Small wooden skewers

1 If using short skewers, thread one mozzarella ball, one tomato, and one whole basil leaf onto each skewer. You can even wrap a basil leaf around a mozzarella ball and skewer it. If using longer skewers, thread two of each onto each stick.

2 Drizzle with olive oil. Sprinkle with sea salt and freshly ground black pepper.

Tip: For more flavor, use garlic-infused olive oil. You can make your own by slowly heating olive oil and sliced garlic in a pan. When edges of garlic start to brown, remove from heat. Let cool to room temperature, and discard garlic slices.

Prep time: *15 minutes,* **Makes** *24 skewers*

Per skewer: 27 calories, 2 g fat, 1 g saturated fat, 2 g protein, 0.4 g carbs, 0.1 g fiber, 0.2 g sugar, 25 mg sodium

Smoked Salmon Quesadillas

Smoked salmon is instantly upscale, but we've made it casual by putting it in a quesadilla. If you're not a fan of goat cheese, use cream cheese instead. You can assemble the quesadillas ahead of time, stack on a plate and chill, covered with plastic wrap, until ready to heat. A cast iron griddle or skillet distributes heat evenly and works well for grilling the quesadillas.

1 (8-oz) pkg smoked salmon, divided into 4 portions

1 (8-oz) log goat cheese, divided into 4 portions

4 tortillas, whole wheat or white

¼ cup Fire-Roasted Red Peppers, thinly sliced (optional)

1 Tbsp fresh chives, chopped

½ cup guacamole, such as Avocado's Number Guacamole, or half of a fresh avocado, sliced

1 Heat skillet over medium-high heat.

2 To assemble quesadillas, spread goat cheese evenly on a tortilla. Place an even layer of salmon on half of the cheese-covered tortilla. Sprinkle red pepper slices and chives on salmon. Fold tortilla in half. Assemble remaining quesadillas.

3 Place quesadillas on hot skillet and toast for 1-2 minutes on each side until tortillas are golden. Cut into triangular wedges.

4 Lightly brush both sides of the quesadillas with oil, or use oil spray. Toast for 1-2 minutes on each side until tortillas are golden and flecked with brown spots from the heat. Cut into triangular wedges.

5 Garnish with guacamole or fresh avocado slices.

Tip: Brush avocado slices with lemon juice to prevent them from browning.

Prep and cooking time: *20 minutes,* **Serves 8**

Per serving: 200 calories, 9 g fat, 4 g saturated fat, 12 g protein, 14 g carbs, 3 g fiber, 0 g sugar, 568 mg sodium

Spicy Tropical Shrimp Boats

All aboard! Shrimp, mango, and jalapeños set sail on endive boats. No utensils needed for this seafood adventure. The sweet flavors in the fruit salsa offset the slightly bitter taste of crunchy endive. Be prepared for the salsa's spicy kick!

1 cup frozen Medium Cooked Tail-Off Shrimp, thawed

½ cup Fire Roasted Papaya Mango Salsa

Salt and pepper

1 head fresh Belgian endive, leaves separated

2 Tbsp refrigerated Cilantro Dressing

Cilantro for garnish

1 Dice shrimp into cubes. Mix shrimp and salsa. Season with salt and pepper to taste.

2 Spoon shrimp mixture onto endive leaves. Arrange shrimp boats on serving platter and drizzle with dressing.

3 Garnish with cilantro.

Variation: For a more traditional (and less spicy) shrimp salad, use ¼ cup Cilantro Dressing or other creamy dressing instead of the fruit salsa. Garnish with cilantro.

Prep time: *15 minutes,* **Serves** *4 (2 boats each)*

Per serving: 101 calories, 3 g fat, 0 g saturated fat, 14 g protein, 5 g carbs, 0 g fiber, 3 g sugar, 524 mg sodium

Indian Spinach Pizza

Tandoori Naan is an Indian flatbread that gets its name from the tandoor (clay oven) in which it is baked. Trader Joe's carries fresh and frozen tandoori naan in a few different flavors. Keep a bag of the frozen tandoori naan in the fridge, and it will come in handy when cooking curry or making this easy ethnic-crossover appetizer. For your own pizza experiments, you can use any of the Indian sauces or curries that Trader Joe's carries, such as the tasty Masala Simmer Sauce.

2 pieces of frozen Tandoori Naan, plain

4 Tbsp Masala Simmer Sauce

1 cup frozen spinach, thawed and drained (squeeze water out with your hands)

2 Tbsp ricotta cheese

½ cup diced tomatoes

1 Preheat oven to 400° F.

2 Spread sauce on top of each naan.

3 Sprinkle on spinach and small pieces of ricotta.

4 Bake for 5 minutes.

5 Remove from oven and top with tomatoes.

Prep time: *5 minutes,* **Hands-off cooking time:** *5 minutes*
Makes 2 small pizzas

Per ½ pizza: 163 calories, 3 g fat, 1 g saturated fat,
6 g protein, 26 g carbs, 2 g fiber, 3 g sugar, 271 mg sodium

Apricot Baked Brie

When Deana was school age, her mom would order a prepared apricot Brie from the specialty grocery store in town, which only stocked it seasonally. She really didn't care for plain Brie back then, but when her mom took that warm, apricot-covered melty concoction out of the oven, she couldn't get enough. Even if you think you don't like Brie, try this baked version; you may not recognize it. This warm and creamy cheese dish is a great accompaniment to some grapes and a bottle of red wine. One night, we had this dish with our Roasted Garlic (page 16) as appetizers and enjoyed it so much that we kept on eating and skipped dinner.

1 (~0.6 lb) wedge Brie cheese, such as Double Crème Brie

2 heaping Tbsp apricot preserves, such as Organic Reduced Sugar Apricot Preserves

1 handful raw sliced almonds

1 Tbsp triple sec (optional)

1 box water crackers

1 Preheat oven to 400° F.

2 Place the wedge of Brie in a small baking dish that is slightly bigger than the Brie. Top with apricot preserves, sprinkle on almonds, and drizzle triple sec over the top.

3 Cover tightly with foil and bake for 12-14 minutes or until cheese is melting. Remove from oven and serve with water crackers. Before your guests attack the Brie unrelentingly, remind them that the dish is hot.

Prep time: *5 minutes*
Hands-off cooking time: *12-14 minutes,* **Serves 8**

Per serving: 181 calories, 10 g fat, 6 g saturated fat, 9 g protein, 13 g carbs, 0 g fiber, 1 g sugar, 254 mg sodium

* Use Savory
Thins crackers

Roasted Garlic (Friends Be Damned)

Roasting mellows out garlic's strong flavor, and it becomes a creamy spread that you can eat on crackers or crusty bread. Our young kids eat it straight from the bulb. Pair with cheese, mix with mashed potatoes, or add to pasta dishes and steaks for great flavor. Garlic aids digestion, boosts immunity, and reduces unhealthy fats and cholesterol in the system. Baking or roasting it whole (or eating it raw, of course, but that's between you and your friends) is the best way to preserve its medicinal properties.

Whole bulbs of garlic
1 Tbsp extra virgin olive oil per bulb
Freshly ground black pepper

1 Preheat oven to 400° F.

2 With a knife, cut tops off garlic bulbs, slicing across tips of cloves. Place each bulb on a square of aluminum foil, drizzle with olive oil, and sprinkle with pepper.

3 Wrap foil around each bulb and toss the wrapped bulbs in the oven (straight on the rack) for 30-40 minutes or until garlic cloves are completely soft and beginning to caramelize. (Just open the foil and take a peek). For a large bulb (2.5 inches across), cooking time will be about 40 minutes.

4 When you gently press at the base of the clove, it will easily squeeze out whole.

Prep time: *5 minutes*
Hands-off cooking time: *40 minutes*
A large bulb serves *4*

Per serving: 36 calories, 4 g fat, 1 g saturated fat,
0 g protein, 1 g carbs, 0 g fiber, 0 g sugar, 2 mg sodium

Prosciutto-Wrapped Scallops

Prosciutto cooks up crisp in the oven and is a nice balance to the soft scallops. Serve these tasty morsels as an appetizer, or as an elegant dinner served on a bed of salad, couscous, risotto, or pilaf.

1 lb large scallops such as New England Wild Jumbo Scallops, thawed (about a dozen scallops)

6 slices prosciutto, cut lengthwise in half

2 Tbsp Green Olive Tapenade or Mixed Olive Bruschetta (optional)

1   Preheat oven to 375° F.

2   Lightly pat scallops dry with a clean paper towel. Season scallops with tapenade, making sure to coat all sides evenly.

3   Wrap each scallop with a band of prosciutto. Place seam side down in a buttered baking dish or cookie sheet. Spread scallops 2 inches apart so that they roast and don't steam.

4   Bake for 15-16 minutes. Do not overcook. Scallops are done when they are opaque and no longer translucent.

Prep time: *10 minutes*
Hands-off cooking time: *15-16 minutes*
Serves *4 (about 3 scallops each)*

Per serving: 147 calories, 4 g fat, 1 g saturated fat,
23 g protein, 4 g carbs, 1 g fiber, 0 g sugar, 677 mg sodium

Goat Cheese Bruschetta Crackers

Quick! You have just a few minutes to whip together an appetizer platter before guests arrive. With a box of crackers, a log of goat cheese, and a container of sun-kissed Fresh Bruschetta Sauce, you can quickly assemble an easy appetizer. To make a casual evening of tasting and mingling, add an array of olives, cheese, crusty breads, our Apricot Baked Brie (page 15), and Roasted Garlic (page 16) to this spread, and serve a bottle of wine.

1 box water crackers

1 (8-oz) log goat cheese

1 container refrigerated Fresh Bruschetta Sauce

1 Place crackers, log of goat cheese, and bowl of bruschetta sauce on a platter.

2 Let guests assemble their own crackers by spreading some goat cheese on a cracker and topping with a small dollop of bruschetta sauce. If you prefer to assemble them all yourself, don't let them sit too long, or they will get soggy.

Tip: For a holiday version with festive colors and flavors, spread goat cheese on crackers and top with a small dollop of Cranberry Apple Butter or Pumpkin Butter, available seasonally.

Prep time: *5 minutes,* **Makes** *about 30 crackers*

Per cracker: 41 calories, 2 g fat, 1 g saturated fat, 1 g protein, 3 g carbs, 0 g fiber, 0 g sugar, 62 mg sodium

G Gluten Free **V** Vegetarian

* Use Savory Thins crackers

Soups and Salads

Arugula Salad with Pine Nuts and Parmesan

This recipe is courtesy of Uncle Bill. Uncle Bill is a wine connoisseur, a restaurateur, and food expert. This is a simple salad and perfect in its simplicity. Measurements aren't necessary. If you love pine nuts, add more pine nuts. If you love Parmesan, then load it on. If you want to make this salad into a light meal, boil some pasta (half a bag of penne) and toss it all together, allowing the arugula to wilt slightly.

1 (7-oz) bag arugula leaves (about 5 cups)

¼ cup extra virgin olive oil

½ cup toasted pine nuts

¾ cup shaved or shredded Parmesan cheese

Juice of ½ lemon

Salt to taste

1 Toss arugula with olive oil until coated.

2 Add pine nuts and Parmesan, and toss lightly.

3 Add lemon juice and season if desired. Toss gently and serve.

Prep time: 5 minutes, **Serves** 4

Per serving: 328 calories, 31 g fat, 6 g saturated fat, 11 g protein, 5 g carbs, 1 g fiber, 1 g sugar, 303 mg sodium

Black Bean Soup

One of our favorites. This soup is a hearty, spicy soup with the warm earthy flavor of cumin and the zing of fresh lime. We like it with tortilla chips on the side. It makes a great meal by itself, or it can be paired with one of our quesadilla recipes for a bigger meal. Not only are black beans high in fiber and folate, but they rival grapes and cranberries for their antioxidant properties. Sensitive to sulfites? Black beans contain the trace mineral molybdenum, which counteracts sulfites. So uncork that bottle of red later tonight.

1 medium yellow onion, chopped, or 1 ½ cups refrigerated Freshly Diced Onion

1 clove garlic, crushed, or 1 cube frozen Crushed Garlic

2 Tbsp extra virgin olive oil

1 tsp ground cumin

2 (15-oz) cans black beans (do not drain)

1 cup (half a 16-oz jar) Chunky Salsa

2 Tbsp lime juice (juice of 1 lime)

Plain yogurt, such as Plain Cream Line Yogurt, or sour cream (optional)

1 In a medium pot, sauté onions in olive oil until they are soft and translucent.

2 Sprinkle in cumin and garlic and sauté for a minute; pour in black beans (including juices), salsa, and lime. Stir to combine and bring to a simmer. Simmer covered for 20 minutes.

3 Ladle soup into individual bowls and top with a dollop of yogurt.

Prep time: *10 minutes,*

Hands-off Cooking time: *20 minutes*

Makes 5 (1-cup) servings

Per serving: 234 calories, 6 g fat, 1 g saturated fat, 9 g protein, 35 g carbs, 9 g fiber, 7 g sugar, 879 mg sodium

Strawberry and Gorgonzola Herb Salad

This delightful spring salad bursts with the flavor of sweet strawberry and the bite of Gorgonzola cheese. If strawberries aren't in season, substitute any fruit of your choice. We love salads that incorporate greens with fruits, nuts, and cheese. Experiment with your own combinations: spinach with cranberries, pine nuts, and goat cheese; arugula with pear, pecans, and blue cheese; the list goes on and on, and they all work with the sweet tang of a simple vinaigrette.

1 (5-oz) bag Herb Salad Mix (about 4 cups)

1 ½ cups fresh sliced strawberries

½ cup Crumbled Gorgonzola cheese

1 cup Mixed Candied Nuts (or use plain/candied walnuts or pecans)

¼ cup bottled Balsamic Vinaigrette (or make your own by mixing 2 parts extra virgin olive oil with 1 part Balsamic vinegar)

1 Combine all ingredients.

2 Toss with of vinaigrette just before serving.

Prep time: *5 minutes,* Serves *4*

Per serving: 355 calories, 31 g fat, 2 g saturated fat, 11 g protein, 13 g carbs, 5 g fiber, 6 g sugar, 299 mg sodium

G Gluten Free V Vegetarian

Spicy Asian Slaw

Jan from Yucaipa, California, won our Chinese New Year's contest with this tasty recipe that combines red cabbage, carrots, cucumber, green onion, and colorful peppers in a flavorful Asian-inspired dressing. We love both the taste and colorful presentation. Try adding chopped romaine leaves for another dimension of color and texture in this pretty salad.

Salad:

1 (10-oz) pkg shredded cabbage (about 7 cups)

1 cup Shredded Carrots

½ English cucumber, quartered and sliced

3 green onions, chopped

½ each of red, yellow, and orange peppers, thinly sliced

Crushed peanuts or sliced almonds (optional)

Dressing:

⅓ cup vegetable oil

2 cloves garlic, crushed, or 2 cubes frozen Crushed Garlic

¼ cup seasoned rice vinegar

2 Tbsp sesame oil

2 Tbsp sugar

½ tsp soy sauce

½-1 tsp chili oil

½ cup cilantro, chopped

Crushed peanuts or sliced almonds (optional)

1 Combine salad ingredients in large bowl.

2 Pour all dressing ingredients into container with tight fitting lid. Shake well to mix.

3 Pour dressing over salad ingredients and chill for 3 hours.

4 Garnish with peanuts or almonds.

Prep time: *15 minutes (make 3 hours ahead of serving time)*
Serves *6*

Per serving: 355 calories, 31 g fat, 2 g saturated fat, 11 g protein, 13 g carbs, 5 g fiber, 6 g sugar, 299 mg sodium

* Use tamari
  instead of
  soy sauce

Asian Dumpling Soup

Here is our version of wonton soup using Asian steam-fried dumplings. In Japan, the dumplings are called gyozas, and in China, they are called *guo tie* (literally meaning "pot stick"), commonly known as potstickers. Most people are familiar with the pan-fried appetizer version, but these dumplings also work really well in soups. Adding a beaten egg at the end creates delicate ribbons reminiscent of egg drop soup.

1 (16-oz) bag frozen gyoza or potstickers

4 cups (one 32-oz carton) low sodium chicken or vegetable broth

1 tsp soy sauce

1 small garlic clove, crushed, or 1 cube frozen Crushed Garlic

3 cups refrigerated Stir Fry Vegetables, any variety, or frozen Stir-Fry Vegetables

1 egg (optional)

1 tsp toasted sesame oil

Black pepper

1 In a medium pot, heat broth, soy sauce, and garlic over medium-high heat. Bring mixture to a boil. Add gyoza and vegetables. When mixture boils again, reduce heat to medium-low and cook for 5 minutes.

2 If using egg, beat with a fork until frothy. Slowly pour into boiling soup in a thin stream, creating cooked ribbons of egg. If you prefer, you can pan-fry the egg and cut into strips or squares. Use as a garnish.

3 Remove from heat. Stir in sesame oil. Sprinkle with black pepper to taste.

Prep and cooking time: *15 minutes,* Serves *4*

Per serving: 245 calories, 7 g fat, 1 g saturated fat, 12 g protein, 32 g carbs, 4 g fiber, 4 g sugar, 813 mg sodium

* Use vegetarian gyoza and broth

Asian Dumpling Soup

Beet and Endive Salad

Take advantage of the ready-to-eat steamed beets available
~~t Trader Joe's to create~~ this elegant salad. Mild red and
topped with colorful beets, candied
t cheese.

ith leaves separated and cut in
ie whole

d and Peeled Baby Beets (½ pkg),

s (or substitute plain walnuts)
ese, in small chunks, or use

ic Vinaigrette or Red Wine & Olive

epper

leaves among 4 salad plates.

2 Top with the beet slices, walnuts, and goat cheese.

3 Drizzle with vinaigrette and season with black
pepper to taste.

Prep time: *10 minutes,* **Serves 4**

*Per serving: 203 calories, 14 g fat, 3 g saturated fat,
4 g protein, 14 g carbs, 3 g fiber, 11 g sugar, 62 mg sodium*

G Gluten Free   **V** Vegetarian

Mediterranean Lentil Salad

Tender precooked lentils make this salad a mix-and-serve breeze. With a light, lemony, fresh taste, this lentil salad is a great side dish or light lunch. Serve with our Olive-Stuffed Bread (page 108). If you have leftovers, place them in tortillas with feta cheese and cucumbers for a healthy wrap.

1 (17.6-oz) pkg refrigerated Steamed Lentils (about 2 ½ cups)

1 ½ cups chopped tomato

½ cup chopped fresh parsley

1 Tbsp fresh mint (optional)

1 Tbsp lemon juice

2 Tbsp extra virgin olive oil

1 Combine lentils, tomatoes, parsley, and mint.

2 Use a fork to whisk lemon juice and olive oil together. Pour dressing over lentils, giving a quick toss to combine.

Prep time: *5 minutes*, Serves *4*

Per serving: 227 calories, 7 g fat, 1 g saturated fat, 14 g protein, 29 g carbs, 11 g fiber, 4 g sugar, 308 mg sodium

Cock-a-Leekie Soup

We love the Scots for coming up with such a great name for a soup! If you ever find yourself at a Robert Burns Night party, this is what they'll serve, along with lots of whiskey. The soup is made of chicken and leeks, with a garnish of parsley and prunes. Prunes? Yes, they really work in this traditional Scottish dish. It's an easy recipe, very healthy, and a great conversation starter. If you like leeks, this is the soup for you.

2 large leeks or 3-4 trimmed leeks (about 8 cups chopped)

2 raw boneless chicken breasts, or use pre-cooked Just Chicken (or cook your own, page 98)

8 cups (two 32-oz cartons) chicken broth

1 lb potatoes, diced into ½-inch cubes (about 3 cups)

1 tsp dried thyme

1 cup milk

Pitted prunes and parsley for garnish

1 Slice leeks in half lengthwise, rinse out any bits of soil, and cut into half-moon slices.

2 In a large pot, add broth and potatoes. Bring to boil, and then lower to a simmer.

3 Toss in leeks and chicken breasts. (If using Just Chicken, add in Step 5) Simmer for 20-25 minutes.

4 Remove chicken breasts and shred or cut into small, bite-size pieces.

5 Add chicken back to pot and add milk. Simmer for a few additional minutes.

6 When serving, top each bowl with 1 Tbsp parsley and 2 thinly sliced prunes.

Prep time: *15 minutes*
Hands-off cooking time: *25-30 minutes*
Serves 6
Per serving: 240 calories, 3 g fat, 1 g saturated fat, 22 g protein, 32 g carbs, 4 g fiber, 12 g sugar, 829 mg sodium

* Choose GF chicken broth

Cozy Butternut Squash Soup

Granted, you can buy good boxed butternut squash soup ready-made at Trader Joe's, but it's almost as easy to make your own. This recipe requires only 10 minutes of active working time and can be tailored a few different ways according to your tastes. The toughest part of the recipe is cutting the squash in half – you need a large, sharp knife for the task. Enjoy this soothing soup on a cold, rainy day.

1 medium-large butternut squash (about 3-4 cups of cooked squash)

1 Tbsp olive oil

3-4 cups chicken or vegetable broth (use as many cups of broth as cups of cooked squash)

½ tsp salt (adjust according to saltiness of broth)

¼ tsp nutmeg

1 Preheat oven to 350° F.

2 Cut squash in half lengthwise, scooping out seeds and strings. Oil each half and place face down on baking sheet. Cook until soft when pierced with knife. Depending on size of squash, cooking time will be roughly 30-50 minutes.

3 Scoop out cooked squash. Add squash and other ingredients to blender, puréeing till smooth.

4 Pour into a large saucepan and heat over medium heat for 10 minutes, but don't allow soup to boil.

Variation: For Curried Butternut Squash Soup, substitute 1 cup light coconut milk for 1 cup of the broth, and substitute ½ tsp curry powder for the nutmeg. Coconut milk is a great way to get creaminess without using heavy cream.

Prep time: *10 minutes,* **Hands-off cooking time:** *40-60 minutes,* **Serves 4**

Per serving: 93 calories, 4 g fat, 1 g saturated fat, 2 g protein, 14 g carbs, 2 g fiber, 3 g sugar, 432 mg sodium

* Choose GF broth

Cream of Broccoli Soup

Do you occasionally indulge in cream of broccoli soup at restaurants, but worry that the cream and butter in the rich soup will clog your arteries? If so, try this lean version. The chunkiness of the soup makes up for the low fat content.

1 (12-oz) bag broccoli florets (4 cups)

1 cup chopped onion or leeks

1 Tbsp olive oil

2 cups chicken or vegetable broth

2 Tbsp butter

2 Tbsp flour

1 cup milk

Salt and pepper to taste

Shredded cheese as garnish (optional)

1 Heat olive oil in a medium sized pot. Cook onions until tender, about 5 minutes.

2 Add broccoli and chicken broth. Cover, reduce heat, and simmer until broccoli is tender, about 10 minutes.

3 While broccoli is cooking, melt butter in a small saucepan. Add flour and cook for a minute, stirring constantly. Add milk and cook until thickened. Add this mixture to the broccoli.

4 Add thickened milk to broccoli, mix thoroughly, and remove from heat. Purée to desired consistency. If using a blender, blend in batches and use force to keep lid on; the heat can make the soup 'explode.'

5 Check soup for seasoning and add salt and pepper as desired. Garnish with cheese and serve immediately.

Prep time: *15 minutes,* **Hands-off cooking time:** *10 minutes,* **Serves** *4*

Per serving: 177 calories, 11 g fat, 5 g saturated fat, 6 g protein, 15 g carbs, 3 g fiber, 7 g sugar, 337 mg sodium

* Use cornstarch instead of flour and choose GF broth

Harvest Grains Vegetable Soup

Harvest Grains is a Trader Joe's bagged combination of Israeli couscous (also known as pearl couscous), red quinoa, baby garbanzo beans, and orzo. It's a wonderful, quick cooking pilaf to use in place of rice. It also makes a satisfying soup that you can customize with your own blend of vegetables. The best part is that it's ready in minutes. For a boost of protein, add frozen cooked shrimp or chunks of cooked chicken during the last few minutes of cooking time. If you have fresh herbs on hand, such as parsley, basil, or thyme, add a tablespoon or two right before you serve the soup.

4 cups (one 32-oz carton) chicken or vegetable broth

1 cup thinly sliced celery

1 cup thinly sliced carrots

½ cup Harvest Grains

Salt and pepper to taste

1 Add broth to a medium saucepan and bring to a boil.

2 Add vegetables and grains. Bring to a boil and simmer for 15 minutes, skimming if needed. Add extra water or broth if soup becomes too thick.

3 Taste and adjust seasonings.

Prep time: *5 minutes*
Hands-off cooking time: *15 minutes, Serves 4*
Per serving: 122 calories, 2 g fat, 0 g saturated fat,
4 g protein, 23 g carbs, 2 g fiber, 4 g sugar, 612 mg sodium

Spicy Shrimp Soup

Mary from Columbia, South Carolina, sent us this wonderful recipe, which combines the flavor of curry and the tang of buttermilk. It's an exotic combination of flavors. Mary normally serves this soup cold, but we liked it equally well warm.

1 ½ lbs small, shelled shrimp

3 Tbsp olive oil

1 small sweet onion, finely diced

1 Tbsp mild curry powder

2 cloves garlic, crushed, or 2 cubes frozen Crushed Garlic

1 (16-oz) bag frozen white corn kernels, thawed

3 cups buttermilk

¼ tsp sea salt

1 tsp freshly ground black pepper

1-2 tsp Tabasco pepper sauce

2 Tbsp freshly minced chives

1 Heat oil over medium heat and sauté onion, curry and garlic until onion is translucent. Add shrimp and sauté until shrimp is just pink - about five minutes. Remove from heat and cool completely.

2 Place 2 cups corn and the buttermilk in food processor and blend until smooth. Transfer to large storage container.

3 Add remaining corn, shrimp mixture, salt and Tabasco, stirring well. Cover and refrigerate for at least 2 hours. Serve soup in chilled bowls, sprinkling top with chives.

Prep and cooking time: *10 minutes,* Serves 4

Per serving: 464 calories, 16 g fat, 3 g saturated fat, 45 g protein, 39 g carbs, 3 g fiber, 10 g sugar, 628 mg sodium

Chicken Tortilla Soup

This warm, flavorful soup is sure to cure the common cold and the common soup. The best part is the contrast of fresh cilantro, fresh avocado, cheese, and crispy chips added at the last minute to this aromatic, spicy soup. It's *delicioso* - make extra!

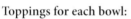

4 boneless chicken thighs

3 cups chicken broth

2 cups water

1 yellow onion, quartered

1 tsp ground cumin

¾ cup Chunky Salsa

2 Tbsp lime juice (juice of 1 lime)

¼ cup chopped fresh cilantro

Toppings for each bowl:

Handful of broken Organic White Corn Tortilla chips or strips

¼ cup Fancy Shredded Mexican Blend cheese

¼ of a ripe avocado, diced

1 Combine water, broth, and onion in a pot and bring to a boil. Add chicken, salsa, and cumin; boil until the chicken is poached, about 10 minutes.

2 Remove large onion pieces and discard. Using two forks, coarsely shred chicken and return to pot.

3 Add lime and simmer for an additional 5 minutes.

4 Remove pot from heat and add cilantro.

5 Ladle soup into individual bowls. Add broken tortilla chips, cheese, and avocado chunks to each bowl. Serve immediately.

Prep and cooking time: *20 minutes*
Serves *4*

Per serving: 383 calories, 25 g fat,
9 g saturated fat, 22 g protein, 20 g carbs,
5 g fiber, 7 g sugar, 977 mg sodium

G Gluten Free

* Choose GF
chicken broth

Roasted Corn and Bean Salad

Roasted corn reminds us of warm summer days, and with Trader Joe's frozen Roasted Corn, you can enjoy the taste of summer year-round. This recipe pairs corn with marinated bean salad, which tastes great right out of the can. If you can't find the bean salad, substitute a can of kidney beans and ¼ cup Italian dressing. Crisp Persian cucumbers round out the texture and complete the salad. They may not always be labeled Persian cucumbers in other parts of the country, but look for small, thin-skinned cucumbers, about 5-6 inches long.

1 (15-oz) can Marinated Bean Salad (entire contents – do not drain)

2 cups frozen Roasted Corn, thawed, or 1 (15-oz) can corn

2 Persian cucumbers, unpeeled, sliced or diced (about 1 heaping cup)

1 Combine all ingredients in salad bowl.

2 Serve chilled. No need for any additional dressing - the marinade from the bean salad is plenty.

Prep time: *5 minutes,* **Serves 4**

Per serving: 215 calories, 2 g fat, 0 g saturated fat,
9 g protein, 42 g carbs, 8 g fiber, 6 g sugar, 361 mg sodium

Sweet Corn and Arugula Salad

Holistic health counselor Marcy Rosenthal sent us this recipe for her favorite summer salad. This fresh and crisp salad bursts with the sweetness of corn and tomato, complemented by the peppery bite of arugula and tang of balsamic. She suggests this salad as a light alternative to classic potato salad, paired wonderfully with a burger or a BLT sandwich (page 75).

1 lb (16-oz) fresh corn kernels, either cut off the cob or frozen sweet corn, thawed

½ bag (3-4 oz) fresh arugula, roughly chopped

½ red onion, diced

1 (1-lb) pkg cherry tomatoes or heirloom mix tomatoes

¼ cup Balsamic Vinaigrette (or make your own, easy recipe below)

Homemade Balsamic Vinaigrette

2 Tbsp extra virgin olive oil

1 Tbsp balsamic vinegar

1 tsp honey

¼ tsp Dijon mustard

1 If using frozen corn, thaw in a strainer under cold water and drain.

2 Combine all salad ingredients in a large bowl. For homemade vinaigrette, whisk together all ingredients for dressing and pour over salad. Toss salad to evenly distribute dressing.

Prep time: *10 minutes*, **Serves 6**

G *Gluten Free* 🌱 *Vegetarian*

Per serving: 119 calories, 3 g fat, 0 g saturated fat, 4 g protein, 23 g carbs, 3 g fiber, 7 g sugar, 33 mg sodium

Souper Fast Alphabet Soup with Meatballs

Food blogger Tracy Holleran gave us this recipe for a playful soup that makes a perfect hot meal for kids (and adults). The practical bonus of this recipe is that all ingredients are either in the pantry or the freezer, so you can make this soup on a moment's notice. Trader Joe's has turkey meatballs for those who avoid red meat.

6 cups chicken or vegetable broth (each 32 oz carton has 4 cups)

1 cup Organic Foursome or other frozen vegetables

¾ cup Organic Alphabet Pasta or pasta of your choice

12 Party-size Mini Meatballs, thawed, or ¾ cup cubed cooked chicken

Grated Parmesan cheese (optional)

1 Heat broth in a saucepan until boiling.

2 Add frozen vegetables and return to a boil.

3 Add pasta, cover slightly, and cook until pasta is just tender.

4 Add meatballs and continue to cook for another 2 minutes or so, until meatballs are heated through and pasta and vegetables are cooked.

5 Serve hot with Parmesan cheese.

Prep and cooking time: *20 minutes,* Serves *4*

Per serving: 191 calories, 9 g fat, 0 g saturated fat, 10 g protein, 19 g carbs, 2 g fiber, 4 g sugar, 1085 mg sodium

* Use Meatless Meatballs or Chicken-less Strips and vegetarian broth

Italian Wedding Soup

Despite common belief, the name for this soup actually has nothing to do with a couple's big day. It refers to the winning combination of greens and meat. In Italian, two things that go well together are said to be "well married," and hence the name for this tasty dish. There are endless variations to Wedding Soup; just make sure meat and greens are involved.

20 frozen Party Size Mini Meatballs (about ½ pkg), or 1 bag frozen Turkey Meatballs, Italian Style Meatballs, or Meatless Meatballs

1 Tbsp extra virgin olive oil

1 small onion, chopped, or 1 cup bagged Freshly Diced Onions

1 clove garlic, crushed, or 1 cube frozen Crushed Garlic

½ cup diced carrots or halved baby carrots

4 cups (one 32-oz carton) chicken or vegetable broth

3 cups fresh Swiss chard, kale, or spinach (if using frozen spinach, use only 1 cup)

¼ cup fresh parsley, chopped

¼ cup grated or shredded Parmesan cheese

1   Heat olive oil over medium-high heat. Add onions, garlic, and carrots. Cook for 5 minutes.

2   Add broth and meatballs. Bring mixture to a boil. Reduce heat and simmer for 20 minutes. Add Swiss chard and boil for 5 minutes longer.

3   Ladle into soup bowls. Garnish with parsley and Parmesan cheese.

Prep time: *15 minutes,*
Hands-off cooking time: *20 minutes*
Serves *4*

* Use Meatless Meatballs and vegetarian broth

Main Meals

Couscous Bowl

This fusion dish takes inspiration from egg fried rice but uses Israeli (pearl) couscous instead of rice. Unlike regular couscous, pearl couscous is a pasta formed into tiny balls, like very small peas. It is toasted, not just dried, which gives it a nutty flavor and a great texture that plays nicely against sauces. If you want to make a regular egg fried rice, substitute cooked rice (brown, white, or a medley). For either this dish or regular egg fried rice, be careful not to overcook the egg or it will become tough and rubbery. Just let it set up and then quickly stir in the other ingredients. The egg will be done cooking by the time you've combined and stir-fried everything else.

1 (12-oz) box of Israeli Couscous (about 1 ⅓ cups)

1 (12-oz) bag broccoli florets (4 cups, with florets cut to bite-size pieces)

2 tsp toasted sesame oil

4 eggs

1 Tbsp olive oil

2 cloves garlic, crushed, or 2 cubes frozen Crushed Garlic

1 ½ cups shelled edamame

1 cup sliced green onion

2 Tbsp soy sauce, Soyaki, or tamari

Extra soy sauce to sprinkle to taste when serving (optional)

1 Prepare couscous according to package instructions, adding broccoli florets to the pot during the last 5 minutes (just toss them on top and put the lid back on). Allow broccoli to steam in the pot along with couscous until both are done.

2 Beat together eggs and sesame oil in a small bowl. In a non-stick skillet or wok, heat olive oil over medium-high heat., and pour eggs into skillet. Eggs will spread out in the pan. Cook only for about 30 seconds, just until it starts to set up, and then use a wooden spatula to push eggs to one side, breaking it up.

3 Quickly toss garlic into the exposed part of the pan. Add couscous and broccoli and stir-fry for an additional minute.

4 Add edamame and green onion. Sprinkle in soy sauce, and stir to combine.

Prep and cooking time: *15-20 minutes*
Serves *4*
Per serving: 441 calories, 15 g fat, 3 g saturated fat,
22 g protein, 52 g carbs, 6 g fiber, 4 g sugar, 663 mg sodium

Anytime Mediterranean Pasta

This pasta dish can be your fallback option any time, even if your fridge is nearly bare. Just keep a bag of pasta, a bag of pine nuts, and a few jarred sauces on hand in your pantry. Parmesan cheese will keep for a long time in your fridge.

8 oz (half a pkg) dry fusilli or penne pasta

½ cup Kalamata olives

2 Tbsp Julienne Sliced Sun Dried Tomatoes

⅓ cup toasted pine nuts

2 Tbsp Pesto alla Genovese Basil Pesto

¼ cup grated or shredded Parmesan cheese

1 Cook pasta according to package instructions and drain.

2 Stir in remaining ingredients, topping with grated Parmesan as desired.

Prep and cooking time: *15 minutes*
Serves *4*

* Use brown
rice pasta

Herb Crusted Fish

Good fish doesn't need much except a little salt and
pepper or a mild seasoning blend. Nothing beats
fresh fish, but Trader Joe's flash-frozen fish is a good
alternative. There's one important thing to remember
when thawing frozen fish: run under cold water. Warm
water ruins the texture of the fish. Nearly any kind/cut
of fish will do for this recipe.

1 lb cod, sole, or other white fish fillets, thawed if frozen

1 egg

2 Tbsp milk

½ cup bread crumbs

1 Tbsp 21 Seasoning Salute (a blend, shelved with spices)

¼ tsp salt

2 Tbsp olive oil

1 In a shallow bowl, beat together egg and milk.

2 On a plate, mix together bread crumbs, seasoning,
and salt.

3 Dip each piece of fish in egg mixture and then coat
with bread crumb mixture.

4 Heat oil in a skillet over medium-high heat. Cook
each piece of fish for just a minute or two on each side.
If fillets are very thick, cook for 3-4 minutes. Do not
overcook fish. Fish is done when it is white and flakes
easily. The outside will be golden and crisp.

Prep and cooking time: *5-10 minutes*

Serves *2*

*Per serving: 488 calories, 22 g fat, 4 g saturated fat, 53 g protein,
20 g carbs, 1 g fiber, 3 g sugar, 648 mg sodium*

Simply Quiche

Forget about that 80's claim that "real men don't eat quiche." Real men don't have hangups about the macho rating of food. Quiche is healthy, sophisticated, and will please any palate. It's a great main dish, from brunch to dinner. It's also easy to make, despite its fancy French culinary roots. Use this recipe as your "foundation recipe," adding ingredients such as cubed ham, sausage, veggies, shrimp, and herbs as you like.

---

1 frozen pie crust, thawed and put into oven-safe pie dish

1 ½ cups crimini mushrooms, chopped or sliced

1 cup half and half

4 eggs

1 cup Quattro Formaggio shredded cheese

½ cup chopped canned or frozen artichoke hearts (not marinated!)

1 cup frozen spinach, thawed and drained (once thawed and drained, it will measure about ¼ cup packed)

⅛ tsp ground nutmeg

¼ tsp salt

---

1 Preheat oven to 375° F.

2 Sauté mushrooms in olive oil just until they start to brown, about 1 minute.

3 Whisk together eggs and half and half. Stir in cheese, artichoke hearts, spinach, nutmeg, and salt.

4 Pour mixture into pie crust and bake for 40 minutes, or until knife inserted into center comes out clean.

5 Allow to cool for a few minutes, then slice and serve.

Prep time: *10 minutes*
Hands-off cooking time: *40 minutes,* Serves 6

Per serving: 286 calories, 20 g fat, 8 g saturated fat, 13 g protein, 15 g carbs, 1 g fiber, 1 g sugar, 529 mg sodium

Go Go Mango Chicken

Chicken is the perfect medium for a great tasting topping; in fact, it's a little boring without it! This recipe is a favorite of adults and kids alike. Mildly spicy salsa and sweet mango chunks form a flavorful, tropically inspired partnership. Serve with Cilantro Jasmine Rice (page 106) or a side of steamed vegetables.

2 skinless, boneless chicken breasts

1 (12-oz) jar Pineapple Salsa

1 ½ cups frozen Mango Chunks or frozen Tropical Fruit Trio

1 Preheat oven to 350° F.

2 Place chicken breasts in a baking dish, cover with salsa, and top with mango chunks (don't bother thawing). Lightly drape with aluminum foil.

3 Bake for 30-40 minutes or until chicken is done and juices run clear when cut. Be careful not to overcook.

Prep time: *5 minutes,* **Hands-off cooking time:** *30-40 minutes,* **Serves 4**

Per serving (½ breast): 181 calories, 2 g fat, 0.5 g saturated fat, 14 g protein, 13 g carbs, 1 g fiber, 5 g sugar, 380 mg sodium

Gluten Free

Sweet and Sour Tofu Stir Fry

The tasty sauce in this stir fry is flavored with layers of honey, soy, and garlic. People have compared it to the "bourbon" sauce popular at some Chinese restaurants. The quick pan frying of the tofu makes the outside crispy and preserves the soft texture inside, a wonderful contrast to the crisp-tender vegetables. Serve over white or brown rice.

½ (19-oz) container regular tofu

¼ cup soy sauce or tamari

¼ cup apple juice

2 Tbsp seasoned rice vinegar

2 Tbsp honey

2 Tbsp ketchup

1 clove garlic, crushed, or 1 cube frozen Crushed Garlic

½ tsp red pepper flakes (optional)

1 tsp cornstarch or flour

2 heads baby bok choy, cut into bite-size pieces (about 2-2 ½ cups)

½ each of yellow, red, and orange bell peppers, sliced

2 cups broccoli florets

2 stalks green onion, sliced

1 Cut tofu into large pieces (such as triangle shapes, about a dozen pieces).

2 In a small saucepan over medium heat, combine soy sauce, juice, vinegar, honey, ketchup, garlic, and pepper flakes. Stir, bring sauce to a simmer, and reduce heat. Add cornstarch (dissolved in 1 Tbsp water) and stir until sauce thickens, about one minute. Set aside.

3 Heat oil in a wok or skillet over high heat. Add tofu and pan-fry until all sides are golden brown. Transfer tofu to a plate and set aside.

4 In the same wok or skillet, over high heat, stir fry thicker white pieces of boy choy, bell pepper, and broccoli, adding 1-2 Tbsp of water to help vegetables cook easily. After 2 minutes, add leafy pieces of bok choy and green onion, stir frying for less than a minute. Add tofu and sauce. Stir to distribute sauce throughout evenly.

Variation: Substitute chicken for tofu. Cut chicken into bite size pieces and pan-fry until cooked through.

Prep and cooking time: *15-20 minutes,* **Serves** *3*

Per serving: 211 calories, 5 g fat,
1 g saturated fat, 11 g protein, 33 g carbs,
4 g fiber, 23 g sugar, 932 mg sodium

* Use tamari instead
of soy sauce, and
cornstarch
instead of flour

Southwest Burrito

A flour tortilla wrapped around black beans, veggies, cheese, and salsa makes a perfect meal for anytime. You'll be surprised at the burst of flavor in this healthy, low-fat burrito.

3 heaping Tbsp canned black beans, drained

A few strips Fire Roasted Red Peppers or Fire Roasted Yellow & Red Peppers

3 Tbsp Fancy Shredded Mexican Blend cheese

2 Tbsp salsa

A few sprigs fresh cilantro

1 large flour tortilla

Slices of fresh avocado (optional)

Dollop of sour cream or yogurt (optional)

1 Place all ingredients down the center of the tortilla.

2 Roll tightly.

Prep time: *5 minutes*
Makes *1 burrito*

G Gluten Free *Vegetarian*

* **Use brown rice tortilla**

Per burrito: 285 calories, 7 g fat, 2 g saturated fat, 14 g protein, 38 g carbs, 4 g fiber, 3 g sugar, 748 mg sodium

Cooking with Trader Joe's cookbook Companion

Tandoori Chicken

Tandoori Chicken gets its name from being cooked in a *tandoor*, a clay oven used for high-heat grilling of meats and flatbreads (like naan, which you can find fresh or frozen at Trader Joe's). We can imitate a *tandoor* by cooking in an oven, set to high heat. Our version of the traditional marinade is made with just two ingredients, Tomato Chutney and yogurt. Serve with Basmati rice and Coconut Curried Vegetables (page 101).

2 leg quarters and 2 split breasts (boneless chicken breasts and thighs are fine too if you prefer)

½ cup plain yogurt

½ cup Tomato Chutney

1 If your chicken pieces are skin on, pull skin off and trim any large pieces of fat.

2 In a large bowl, mix yogurt and chutney.

3 Add chicken and move around to coat all pieces. Cover and refrigerate for at least 4 hours and up to overnight.

4 Preheat oven to 400° F. Place chicken pieces (which will be coated in marinade) in a glass baking dish. Bake uncovered for about 35-40 minutes or until juices run clear when chicken is pierced. If using boneless pieces, baking time will be closer to 25 minutes. Baking time will vary depending on thickness of chicken.

Note: If you're a fan of the typical day-glo red color of tandoori chicken, add 1 tsp paprika to the marinade. (Many restaurants actually use food coloring.) For a little extra heat, add ½ tsp cayenne or chili powder to the marinade.

Prep time: *5-10 minutes (not counting marinating time)*
Hands-off cooking time: *40 minutes,* **Serves 4**

Per serving: 277 calories, 8 g fat, 2 g saturated fat, 37 g protein, 12 g carbs, 0 g fiber, 10 g sugar, 476 mg sodium

Gluten Free

Greek Chicken Stew

With slow-cooked and tender chicken, olives, vegetables, and a tangy tomato base...it's a real comfort food. Besides tasting great, it's easy to make in large batches, is even better the next day, and freezes nicely. The stew base is a mirepoix. "Mirepoix" sounds ultra fancy, but it's simply the French reference to the chopped and sautéed combination of onions, celery, and carrots, "the holy trinity" of French cuisine. Trader Joe's carries mirepoix, chopped and ready in the produce section. The chopping is not difficult, but using the ready-to-use mirepoix makes this recipe even easier.

2 lbs skinless, boneless chicken breasts (~4 breasts)

¼ cup flour

½ tsp salt

½ tsp pepper

1 tsp dried oregano

2 Tbsp olive oil, divided

1 (14.5-oz) container Mirepoix, or 1 cup each chopped onion, celery, and carrots

1 clove garlic, crushed, or 1 cube frozen Crushed Garlic

1 (14.5-oz) can no salt added diced tomato

2 cups chicken broth

¼ cup dry white wine

1 (12-oz) jar pitted Kalamata olives, drained

1 Preheat oven to 350° F.

2 Combine flour, salt, pepper, and oregano. Coat chicken pieces with this mixture.

3 Heat a pan with 1 Tbsp oil. Brown chicken on both sides, and then transfer to a deep baking dish or casserole. Sprinkle remaining flour mixture over chicken.

4 Add 1 Tbsp oil to the same pan and sauté onions, celery, and carrots. Stir often and cook until onions are soft, adding garlic during the last few minutes.

5 Add diced tomatoes (including juices), tomato paste, broth, wine, and olives. Stir well, and bring to a simmer for a few minutes. Pour this mixture over chicken.

6 Cover dish tightly with a lid or with foil, and bake for up to 2 hours. Chicken will be cooked after the first 40 minutes, but the longer baking time will meld the sauce and give it that long-cooked quality.

7 Serve over quinoa, basmati rice, or noodles.

Prep time: *20 minutes*
Hands-off cooking time: *2 hours*
Serves 8

Per serving (½ breast): 292 calories, 15 g fat, 1 g saturated fat, 27 g protein, 14 g carbs, 3 g fiber, 5 g sugar, 436 mg sodium

G Gluten Free * Omit flour (sprinkle chicken with salt, pepper oregano) and choose gluten-free broth

Chutney-Stuffed Chicken

The recipe title makes this dish sound more complex than it really is. A simple yogurt-based marinade tenderizes the chicken and makes for great oven-baked chicken breasts. Before baking, a slit is made in the breast and filled with sweet and spicy ready-made chutney. The chutney stuffing creates a tantalizing presentation and a burst of flavor in every bite. Alternatively, cut the chicken into kabobs, serving the chutney as a dipping sauce.

2 boneless skinless chicken breasts

1 cup yogurt

1 tsp Spanish Saffron

½ medium onion, cut in thin slices

½ tsp salt

½ tsp pepper

¼ cup of your favorite chutney, such as Apple Cranberry Chutney or Mango Ginger Chutney

1 Combine yogurt, saffron, onion, salt, and pepper. Let marinade sit for a few minutes to allow saffron to soften up, and then stir marinade until it is a bright yellow. Add chicken to marinade. Make sure chicken is well coated on all sides, and place in fridge for at least 5 hours.

2 Preheat oven to 350° F.

3 Remove chicken from marinade and slice a deep pocket along sides of each breast. Stuff each breast with 2 Tbsp chutney. Bake for 30-35 minutes, depending on thickness of breasts.

Note: For kabobs, push chicken chunks onto skewers and cook for about 15-20 minutes in a preheated 400° F oven or for 10 minutes under the broiler. Even better, use your grill.

Prep time: *10 minutes (not counting marinating time)*
Hands-off cooking time: *30-35 minutes,* **Serves 4**

Per serving (½ breast): 163 calories, 2 g fat,
0 g saturated fat, 26 g protein, 10 g carbs, 0.5 g fiber,
8 g sugar, 136 mg sodium

Almond-Crusted Pork Tenderloin

Helen from Seattle won first prize in one of our recipe contests with this easy recipe for pork tenderloin. We loved the sweet, smoky, and tangy flavors as well as the contrast of the crunchy almond crust to the juicy meat. Trader Joe's pork comes conveniently packaged in individual 1-lb tenderloins in the refrigerated case.

....

1 lb pork tenderloin

2 Tbsp Soyaki

2 Tbsp orange marmalade or fruit preserves

2 cloves garlic, minced

1 tsp cumin

2 Tbsp almonds, coarsely chopped

....

1 In a small bowl, combine Soyaki, marmalade, garlic, and cumin.

2 Preheat oven to 425° F. Place pork in a shallow dish and coat on all sides with marinade. Marinate 10 - 20 minutes.

3 Roll pork in chopped almonds and place on a rack over a foil-lined baking dish. Bake for 25 minutes. Cover with foil the final 10 minutes if almonds turn dark brown.

4 Remove from heat, and cover with foil if you haven't already. Allow pork to rest 5 minutes before cutting to preserve juiciness.

Prep time: *5 minutes (not including 10-20 minutes of marinating time)*
Hands-off cooking time: *25 minutes,* **Serves** *4*

Per serving: 220 calories, 9 g fat, 2 g saturated fat, 25 g protein, 10 g carbs, 0 g fiber, 8 g sugar, 305 mg sodium

Fiery Mango Mahi-Mahi

Mahi-mahi, also called dorado or dolphinfish, is a very popular item on restaurant menus due to its excellent flavor and firm texture. We're keeping things simple with a few good ingredients to highlight the fish. Save time by using pre-made fruit salsa, but be warned that this one has a very spicy kick of jalapeño. For milder palates, use another fruit salsa or make your own. Look for U.S. or Hawaii caught mahi-mahi.

4 frozen mahi mahi fillets, thawed

2 tsp olive oil

1 tsp fresh lemon juice

2 cups refrigerated Fire Roasted Papaya Mango Salsa

Dash salt

¼ tsp black pepper

1 Preheat grill pan or sauté pan on high heat.

2 Mix olive oil and lemon juice, and drizzle mixture over fish, turning to coat all sides. Season with salt and pepper. Cook fish 3 minutes on each side. Take care not to overcook mahi-mahi, else it will become tough and rubbery. As soon as fish becomes opaque, remove from heat to prevent overcooking.

3 Top each fish fillet with ½ cup of fruit salsa. Serve with additional salsa on the side.

Prep and cooking time: *10 minutes,* Serves *4*

Per serving: 151 calories, 3 g fat, 0 g saturated fat,
21 g protein, 7 g carbs, 0 g fiber, 4 g sugar, 549 mg sodium

Hurry for Curry

Curry sauces are complex and delicious, and they are a great way to creatively use leftover ingredients. Although bottled Thai Yellow Curry already has coconut milk in it, adding more coconut milk softens and delicately sweetens the curry. Light Coconut Milk is also easy on the calories; unlike heavy cream, coconut milk has 50 calories per $\frac{1}{3}$ cup. Not too bad for a little added creaminess. Feel free to substitute whatever vegetables you have on hand. Serve with rice, couscous, or tandoori naan.

1 (11-oz) bottle Thai Yellow Curry

¾ cup Light Coconut Milk (about half the can)

1 (16-oz) container firm tofu, cut into bite-size pieces

1 ½ cups green beans, cut into 2-inch pieces

1 red bell pepper, cut into bite-size pieces

½ onion, cut into bite-size pieces

½ cup baby carrots or sliced carrots

½ cup mushrooms, halved or quartered

1 Tbsp fresh basil leaves, chopped

1 Pour curry and coconut milk into medium-sized saucepan. Stir to combine.

2 Add tofu and vegetables. Bring to a boil, reduce heat to simmer, and cook 10-12 minutes, or until vegetables are crisp-tender.

3 Stir in basil and remove from heat. Serve over steamed jasmine rice or brown rice.

Prep time: *10 minutes*, Hands-off cooking time: *10-12 minutes*, Serves 6

Per serving: 293 calories, 18 g fat, 6 g saturated fat, 13 g protein, 24 g carbs, 5 g fiber, 10 g sugar, 1067 mg sodium

(Just Like Your Mawmaw's) Shrimp Creole

Shrimp creole is made using a roux, which is the starting base for most Cajun/Creole stews, soups, and sauces. A roux is a simple thickener made by mixing equal amounts of flour and fat. Combine the two and cook in a pan, stirring constantly. The longer you cook it, the darker and nuttier-tasting it gets. This recipe for shrimp creole is from scratch, but it's relatively simple and easy to make. It does involve a bit of stirring and hovering, but that's a great opportunity to share a glass of wine with someone.

1 lb peeled and cleaned jumbo shrimp, fresh or frozen

½ cup vegetable oil

½ cup all-purpose flour

1 medium onion, chopped

1 green bell pepper, chopped (about 1 ½ cups)

1 ½ cups chopped celery

1 clove garlic, crushed, or 1 cube frozen Crushed Garlic

½ tsp dried thyme

1 bay leaf

2 cups chicken broth or vegetable stock

1 cup dry white wine

¼ tsp cayenne or chili powder

2 cups fresh tomato, chopped, or one (14.5-oz) can diced tomatoes

3 Tbsp tomato paste

1 To make roux, pour vegetable oil into a large skillet or other flat bottomed pan over medium-low heat. Slowly add flour, whisking it into the oil. Stir roux constantly until it reaches a peanut butter color or a milk chocolate brown (about 15 minutes).

2 Add onion, pepper, and celery and cook for an additional 5 minutes until vegetables are soft. The roux will have continued to darken a bit.

3 Add garlic, thyme, bay leaf, broth, wine, cayenne, tomato, and tomato paste. Stir until tomato paste has dissolved and the sauce is smooth. Simmer for 30 minutes. Add a little broth or wine if necessary to maintain fluidity.

4 Meanwhile, cook some rice. If using frozen shrimp, thaw shrimp by running under cold water. Pull tails off by pinching between your thumb and index finger, giving a squeeze.

5 Add shrimp and cook for an extra 10 minutes, or just until shrimp are pink and curled. Remove bay leaf. Serve immediately over rice.

Prep time: *25 minutes,* **Cooking time:** *40 minutes,* **Serves** *4*

Per serving: 529 calories, 30 g fat, 4 g saturated fat, 27 g protein, 27 g carbs, 3 g fiber, 6 g sugar, 502 mg sodium

Eggplant Parmesan

Eggplant Parmesan, also known as *melanzane alla parmigiana* or *eggplant parmigiana*, is a well-loved classic Italian dish originating in Naples. The time-consuming part of a traditional eggplant Parmesan recipe is the preparation of the eggplant cutlets – they need to be salted, allowed to sit, rinsed, then breaded and fried. With Trader Joe's frozen eggplant cutlets, suddenly the recipe a snap. Use your favorite marinara, try different cheeses (such as fresh mozzarella or ricotta cheese), add a bag of thawed frozen spinach, or add fresh herbs to your liking. Serve with a green salad and crusty bread.

1 (1-lb) box Eggplant Cutlets
1 (25-oz) jar Organic Marinara Sauce
1 ½ cups shredded Mozzarella cheese
½ cup shredded Parmesan cheese
Chopped fresh basil or parsley (optional)

1 Preheat oven to 375° F.

2 In the bottom of an 8x10 or 9x12-inch baking dish, spread one cup of marinara. Place frozen eggplant cutlets in the dish in one layer, overlapping as necessary.

3 Pour remaining marinara over eggplant cutlets, then sprinkle with the two cheeses.

4 Bake uncovered for 35 minutes. Remove from oven and let rest 5-10 minutes. Top with fresh herbs before serving.

Prep time: *5 minutes,* **Hands-off cooking time:** *35 minutes,* Serves 8

Per serving: 241 calories, 12 g fat, 4 g saturated fat, 12 g protein, 22 g carbs, 2 g fiber, 11 g sugar, 528 mg sodium

Lemon Sole

Sole is a delicate white fish with a clean flavor. A burst of lemon brightens this dish with a punch of flavor. If you don't care for fish, you may substitute chicken; pounding the chicken to a thin fillet will help it cook faster.

1.5 lbs sole fillets

½ cup white flour

½ tsp salt

¼ tsp black pepper

1 Tbsp extra virgin olive oil

1 Tbsp butter

1 cup chicken broth

¼ cup fresh lemon juice

2 teaspoons jarred capers (optional)

1 Heat olive oil and butter in a large nonstick skillet over medium-high heat.

2 Sprinkle fish with salt and pepper. Coat with flour, shaking off excess. Cook for 3 minutes on each side or until golden brown. Transfer fish to a plate while you make the lemon sauce, and return skillet to heat.

3 Mix chicken broth, lemon juice, and capers. Add broth mixture to the same skillet used to cook fish, stirring to loosen browned bits. Bring to a boil and cook 3 minutes. Sauce will thicken slightly.

4 Pour sauce over fish and serve. Garnish with wedges of fresh lemon.

Prep and cooking time: *15 minutes,* **Serves** *4*

Per serving: 226 calories, 9 g fat, 3 g saturated fat, 25 g protein, 12 g carbs, 0 g fiber, 0 g sugar, 493 mg sodium

Classic Lasagna

Lasagna is one of the most popular one-dish meals of all time. It's great for large groups, can be assembled in advance, and freezes well. No-boil lasagna noodles are a great time-saver, eliminating the need for pre-cooking the pasta. For a twist on classic lasagna, try using cottage cheese instead of ricotta, for more texture and flavor. Serve lasagna with Garlic Bread (page 114).

1 pkg (1-1.3 lb) ground turkey or beef

9 sheets no-boil lasagna noodles

1 Tbsp olive oil

1 medium onion, chopped

1 (8-oz) pkg sliced mushrooms (optional)

6 cups marinara sauce (about a jar and a half, or more if you like extra sauce)

¼ cup fresh basil, chopped, or 1 Tbsp dried basil

1 Tbsp sugar

1 (12-oz) pkg ricotta cheese or cottage cheese

¼ cup grated Parmesan cheese

1 egg

8 oz (half a bag) frozen spinach, thawed and excess water squeezed out

3 cups shredded mozzarella

1   Preheat oven to 350° F.

2   Heat a deep skillet over medium-high heat. Add olive oil and onion. Cook for 5 minutes.

3   Add turkey and cook until browned. If using mushrooms, add in last 5 minutes and cook, stirring frequently.

4   Add marinara sauce, basil, and sugar, and stir well. Remove from heat. You don't need to cook the sauce as it will cook in the oven.

5 In a bowl, mix cottage cheese, Parmesan, egg and spinach.

6 Cover bottom of a 9x13-inch baking pan with 1 cup of marinara sauce. Add a layer of 3 lasagna noodles. Spread ½ of the cottage cheese mixture evenly over noodles. Pour ⅓ of the marinara sauce on top and spread evenly. Sprinkle with 1 cup mozzarella cheese. Top with another layer of 3 noodles, cottage cheese, marinara, and mozzarella. The final layer is remaining noodles, marinara sauce, and mozzarella.

7 Bake, covered with foil, for 30 minutes. Remove foil and bake for an additional 15 minutes. Let lasagna cool for a few minutes before serving, so that it holds its shape better (and your guests will appreciate not burning the roofs of their mouths). Garnish with additional chopped basil if desired.

Prep time: *20 minutes*
Hands-off cooking time: *45 minutes,* **Serves 8**

Per serving: 454 calories, 17 g fat, 7 g saturated fat, 46 g protein, 31 g carbs, 5 g fiber, 11 g sugar, 822 mg sodium

* Omit meat; substitute with meatless product or sliced vegetables such as zucchini or eggplant

Barbecue Chicken Pasta

Pasta and barbecue lovers alike will love the combination of flavors in this dish. On the surface, it may look like regular pasta and tomato sauce, but the subtle barbecue flavors play on your palate, giving this dish a great depth of flavor. If you prefer more sauce in your pasta, feel free to go heavier on the marinara/BBQ sauces. Don't skip the cilantro – it adds to the party of flavors in this dish.

8 oz (half a bag) farfalle pasta, or other pasta of your choice

1 Tbsp extra virgin olive oil

2 cups chicken, cut into bite-size pieces (or pre-cooked Just Chicken, or make your own, page 98)

1 cup frozen Melange à Trois bell pepper strips, or 1 bell pepper, cut into strips

1 clove garlic, crushed, or 1 cube frozen Crushed Garlic

1 cup marinara sauce

½ cup barbecue sauce

½ cup Quattro Formaggio Shredded Cheese

¼ cup cilantro, chopped

1 Cook pasta according to package instructions.

2 Meanwhile, heat olive oil in a large nonstick skillet over medium heat. Add chicken and sauté 5 minutes, until chicken is nearly cooked through. Add vegetables and garlic, and cook 3 minutes more. Add marinara and barbecue sauce and heat just to boiling. Remove from heat.

3 Drain pasta, reserving ¼ cup starchy pasta water to thin out the sauce. Add chicken mixture and cheese. Toss to coat.

4 Top with cilantro and serve.

G Gluten Free

Vegetarian

* Use brown rice pasta * Use Chicken less Strips

Prep and cooking time: *20 minutes*
Serves 4

Per serving: 477 calories, 14 g fat, 4 g saturated fat, 32 g protein, 62 g carbs, 5 g fiber, 15 g sugar, 677 mg sodium

Lime Grilled Chicken

Our favorite chicken marinade is also one of the simplest to make. Lime, saffron, and onion...that's it! It's a popular marinade in the Middle East. The high acidity of this marinade penetrates the chicken and tenderizes it quickly. Use the same marinade for chicken kabobs. Serve with grilled vegetables, Trader Joe's lavash bread, basmati rice, and Raita (page 115).

4 skinless, boneless chicken breasts (about 2 lbs)

1 cup fresh lime juice (or any combination of lime and/or lemon juice)

1 tsp ground Spanish Saffron

1 small yellow onion, very thinly sliced

2 Tbsp melted butter or olive oil

1 Combine lime, saffron, and onion. Marinate chicken in mixture for 1-3 hours.

2 Remove chicken from marinade and brush with melted butter to seal in juices. Dispose of used marinade.

3 Cook on the grill for about 5-7 minutes per side. Cook until juices run clear when pierced. Alternatively, you can press on the chicken to test for doneness. The chicken will feel springy (but not soft) when done.

Prep time: 5-10 minutes (plus 1 hour time to marinate the chicken)

Hands-off cooking time: *15 minutes,* **Serves 8**

G *Gluten Free*

Per serving (½ breast): 155 calories, 4 g fat, 2 g saturated fat, 25 g protein, 2 g carbs, 0 g fiber, 1 g sugar, 61 mg sodium

Vegetarian Mushroom Moussaka

This moussaka is a streamlined, quicker version of one in Mollie Katzen's *Moosewood Cookbook*. It's a hearty meal that will satisfy even meat-lovers. The only part of this recipe that requires some fussing is the eggplant preparation, but it's well worth it. The classic version of moussaka is topped with bechamel sauce, a creamy white sauce. But we couldn't really bring ourselves to top off all those healthy ingredients with fat and flour, so we've captured the flavors of the bechamel sauce by making a sauce out of yogurt, nutmeg, and Parmesan. It's so delicious, you won't miss the fat.

3 large eggplants, unpeeled and sliced into thin ¼-inch rounds.

2 trimmed leeks, chopped (about 3 cups)

1 (10-oz) bag sliced Crimini mushrooms

1 (24-oz) jar Rustico Southern Italian Sauce

1 tsp cinnamon

1 packed cup chopped parsley

½ cup shredded Parmesan cheese

For the sauce:

1 cup yogurt

¼ tsp nutmeg

½ cup shredded Parmesan cheese

1 Salt eggplant slices, making sure both sides are lightly covered, and place in a colander. Let sit for at least 15 minutes, preferably 30.

2 Preheat oven to 450° F. Add 1 Tbsp olive oil to a deep skillet over medium-high heat. Sauté leeks for 4 minutes. Add mushrooms and sauté for an additional 3-4 minutes. Add sauce and cinnamon. Bring to a simmer and then remove from heat. Stir in parsley and Parmesan.

3   Rinse eggplant slices and pat dry. Brush slices with olive oil and then spread on two baking sheets. Roast in oven for about 15 minutes until slices look softened.

4   Reduce oven to 375º F. Oil an 8x12 or 9x13-inch baking dish. Place two layers of eggplant slices in the bottom and add mushroom sauce on top. Cover with remaining eggplant slices (another two layers).

5   In a small bowl, mix yogurt, nutmeg, and Parmesan. Pour this over top of casserole and spread evenly.

6   Bake casserole, uncovered, for 40 minutes. Remove from oven and let rest 5 minutes before serving.

Prep time: *20 minutes, plus 15-30 minutes for salted eggplant to sit and sweat*
Hands-off cooking time: *15 + 40 minutes,* **Serves 8**

Per serving: 174 calories, 5 g fat, 3 g saturated fat, 12 g protein, 24 g carbs, 9 g fiber, 13 g sugar, 580 mg sodium

Enchilada Casserole

Instead of meticulously rolling enchiladas, throw everything in a pan, lasagna-style, for an easy enchilada casserole. Make your own enchilada sauce using a simple combination of salsa and sour cream. You can't get any easier than that! Add your own variations to this basic recipe, such as bell peppers, sliced olives, or corn.

3 cups cooked chicken, shredded or chopped

9 corn tortillas

1 (15-oz) can black beans, rinsed and drained

1 jar Chunky Salsa (approx 2 cups)

1 cup sour cream

1 cup chopped tomatoes

1 cup Fancy Mexican Blend shredded cheese

¼ cup chopped cilantro

Avocado chunks (optional)

1 Preheat oven to 350º F. Lightly grease a 9x13-inch pan.

2 Mix salsa and sour cream. Spread a few spoonfuls in bottom of baking pan. Place 3 tortillas in pan, overlapping/trimming as necessary. Top with 1 cup chicken, ⅓ of the beans, and ⅓ of the salsa mixture. Create two more layers in that order: tortillas, chicken, beans, and salsa mixture. (Note: you can add extra cheese in the layers for a cheesier casserole.)

3 Spread tomatoes evenly on top. Sprinkle with shredded cheese.

4 Bake for 30-40 minutes or until bubbling hot.

5 Remove from heat and sprinkle cilantro and avocados on top.

Prep time: *15 minutes*

Hands-off cooking time: *30-40 minutes,* **Serves** 6

Per serving: 435 calories, 20 g fat, 10 g saturated fat, 31 g protein, 37 g carbs, 5 g fiber, 3 g sugar, 798 mg sodium

 * Use Chicken-less Strips, or add an extra can of beans and extra cheese instead of chicken

Spinach Pesto Pasta Salad

The most popular flavors of Italy are combined in this colorful pasta salad. The pesto, cherry tomatoes, pine nuts, and mozzarella balls complement the freshness of baby spinach. It is a convenient make-ahead dish for a large crowd. You can use any pasta variety, including brown rice pasta.

1 (16-oz) bag fusilli pasta

1 (7-oz) container of refrigerated Genova Pesto

3 oz (½ bag) baby spinach

1 (16-oz) container heirloom cherry tomato mix

½ cup toasted pine nuts

1 (8-oz) container Ciliegine fresh mozzarella balls, drained

1 In a large pot, boil pasta in salted water according to instructions on bag. Drain completely.

2 In a large bowl, add pasta and pesto. Stir to distribute pesto throughout the pasta. Add spinach, tomatoes, pine nuts, and mozzarella balls. Stir gently to combine.

Prep and cooking time: *15 minutes*
Serves *8*

Per serving: 456 calories, 24 g fat, 4 g saturated fat, 14 g protein, 51 g carbs, 5 g fiber, 0 g sugar, 104 mg sodium

* Use brown rice pasta

Turkish Minted Kabobs

This recipe uses warm spices like cumin and cinnamon to add intense flavor to meat, but without any heat. A friend gave us a traditional Turkish recipe, but we didn't own half the spices and decided to try it with just what was on hand, and we haven't gone back. These kabobs are wonderful with lamb or beef. Serve on a bed of couscous or Middle Eastern lavash bread, with a side of our Raita (page 115). It's also great with the Sweet and Tart Cherry Rice recipe in our first cookbook, *"Cooking with All Things Trader Joe's."*

2 lbs leg of lamb (or beef), cut into 1-inch chunks

2 tsp cumin

1 tsp cinnamon

1 tsp salt

½ tsp black pepper

5 cloves garlic, crushed, or 5 cubes frozen Crushed Garlic

2 Tbsp olive oil

¼ cup chopped fresh mint or 1 Tbsp dried mint

1 red onion, cut into 1-inch chunks

1   Combine all spices, garlic, oil, and mint in a Ziploc bag (everything except meat and onion). Massage with your hands until all spices are well combined. The spice mixture will be thick in texture, like a rub or paste.

2   Add meat and continue to massage, coating each piece of meat with spice mixture. Marinate in refrigerator for 2 hours or overnight..

3   Skewer meat and onion chunks. Depending on the size of your skewers, you will have 4-6 skewers.

4   Grill or pan-fry for 6-8 minutes total, turning skewers every couple of minutes.

5   Let meat rest under foil for 10 minutes before serving.

Prep time: *15 minutes (not including marinating time),* **Cooking time:** *6-8 minutes,* **Serves 4**

Per serving: 537 calories, 38 g fat, 14 g saturated fat, 43 g protein, 5 g carbs, 1 g fiber, 1 g sugar, 756 mg sodium

Peachy Quesadilla

Trader Joe's Peach Salsa is a great combination of sweet, spicy, and smoky flavors. It's the perfect highlight to this very simple meal that's an easy lunch for one or a quick meal on the run. This is an overstuffed quesadilla with cheese, fresh tomatoes, microgreens, and Peach Salsa to add a splash of flavor.

1 medium tortilla

½ cup Shredded 3 Cheese Blend

½ cup chopped tomatoes

½ cup loose Organic Microgreens

2 Tbsp Peach Salsa

1 Place tortilla in a skillet over medium-high heat. Sprinkle with cheese.

2 When cheese has melted, put tortilla on a plate. Fill one side with tomatoes, microgreens, and salsa. Fold over.

Prep and cooking time: *5-10 minutes*
Makes *1 quesadilla*

* **Use brown rice tortilla**

Per quesadilla: 347 calories, 19 g fat, 10 g saturated fat, 19 g protein, 29 g carbs, 5 g fiber, 4 g sugar, 570 mg sodium

Easy Shepherd's Pie

Shepherd's pie, also known as cottage pie, is a layered casserole traditionally made with lamb or mutton, topped with a crust made of mashed potatoes. It's a comforting one-dish meal, and a favorite in our household. There are many directions you can take this dish based on what you have in your fridge. Toss mushrooms in with the meat, or broccoli or cauliflower florets in with the vegetables. It's a great way to use up leftover meats and vegetables, so feel free to substitute at will!

1 pkg (1-1.3 lb) pkg ground turkey or beef

1 Tbsp olive oil

1 medium onion, chopped

1 ½ cups Turkey Gravy, available in a box, or make your own* (recipe below)

1 (16-oz) pkg frozen vegetables, thawed

1 (28-oz) pkg frozen Mashed Potatoes, prepared, or make your own using 4 russet potatoes, boiled and then mashed with milk, butter, and salt

¾ cup shredded cheddar cheese

*Quick gravy (instructions included in step #4) using these 3 ingredients:

2 Tbsp flour

½ cup milk

1 cup chicken broth

1   Preheat oven to 375° F.

2   Heat olive oil in a medium-size fry pan. Add onions
    and cook until softened, about 5 minutes.

3   Add ground turkey and cook until browned, about
    10 minutes.

4   If using boxed Turkey Gravy, pour into cooked turkey
    and stir until combined. If making your own sauce,
    add flour to turkey, and cook 1 minute longer, stirring
    frequently. Add milk and chicken broth, cooking
    for 2-3 minutes until sauce thickens. Check for
    seasonings and add salt and pepper to taste.

5   Pour turkey mixture into bottom of a baking dish.
    Sizes that work well are 9x9-inch or 8x10-inch. Top
    with vegetables, and then mashed potatoes. Sprinkle
    cheese on top.

6   Bake for 20-30 minutes until cheese is melted and
    casserole is bubbling.

Prep time: *20 minutes*
Hands-off cooking time: *20-30 minutes,* Serves *6*

*Per serving: 367 calories, 10 g fat, 5 g saturated fat, 31 g protein,
39 g carbs, 3 g fiber, 5 g sugar, 863 mg sodium*

Seared Ahi Tuna on Lemon Pappardelle

This is one of those meals that looks ultra-fancy, but it's really a snap to make. Lemon Pepper provides a flavorful crust of black peppercorns, sea salt, onion, lemon, and garlic. For a lighter meal, serve the ahi on a baby salad mix tossed in vinaigrette.

2 Sashimi Grade Ahi Tuna steaks (6-8 oz each)

1 (8-oz) pkg Lemon Pepper Pappardelle pasta

1 Tbsp Lemon Pepper grinds

2 tsp + 1 Tbsp olive oil

1 Tbsp freshly squeezed lemon juice

Pinch of salt

1 Tbsp chopped parsley or basil

1 Cook pasta according to package instructions.

2 Heat 2 tsp olive oil in a nonstick skillet over medium to high heat.

3 Coat all sides of the tuna steaks with lemon pepper seasoning. When pan is hot, sear both sides of the tuna steaks for 1-2 minutes per side. (2 minutes per side for medium-rare, cook less for more rare.)

4 Remove tuna from pan and slice into ¼-inch slices.

5 Mix remaining 1 Tbsp olive oil with lemon juice and salt to make a quick dressing. Toss the drained pasta in the dressing.

6 Serve tuna slices over pasta and sprinkle with chopped parsley.

Prep and cooking time: *10 minutes,* **Serves** *4*

Per serving: 471 calories, 8 g fat, 1 g saturated fat, 37 g protein, 57 g carbs, 3 g fiber, 2 g sugar, 412 mg sodium

Chipotle Turkey Chili

On a cold night, warm your body and soul with a big bowl of homemade chili. Refried beans thicken the chili, giving it long-cooked texture and flavor in just minutes. Chipotle salsa adds a kick of heat, while a splash of barbecue sauce balances the spice with a touch of smoky sweetness.

1 (~1.3 lb) pkg ground turkey or beef

1 medium onion, chopped, or 1 ½ cups bagged Freshly Diced Onions

1 Tbsp olive oil

1 tsp ground cumin

1 (28-oz) can diced tomatoes

1 (15-oz) can black beans

¾ cup refried black or pinto beans (half the can, or use entire can for thicker chili)

½ cup Chipotle Salsa

¼ cup barbecue sauce

Sour cream (optional)

Fancy Shredded Mexican Blend cheese (optional)

1 Heat olive oil in medium saucepan over medium heat. Cook onions 5 minutes. Add ground turkey and cook until brown, breaking it up as it cooks. Add ground cumin and cook 1 minute longer.

2 Add remaining ingredients. Refried beans need to be broken up and stirred into the chili until dissolved.

3 When chili comes to a boil, lower heat and simmer for 10 minutes.

4 Garnish with sour cream and cheese.

Prep time: *10 minutes*
Hands-off cooking time: *15 minutes,* **Serves** *4*

Per serving: 387 calories, 4 g fat, 0 g saturated fat, 44 g protein, 40 g carbs, 7 g fiber, 11 g sugar, 913 mg sodium

Soyaki Broiled Salmon

This is a twist on Teriyaki salmon. Dijon mustard adds a zing that will make ordinary Teriyaki sauces seem rather run-of-the-mill. If you've never used your broiler (yes, most ovens come with one built in), this is a good recipe to test it on. Cooking salmon under the high heat of a broiler will create a crusty top layer and lock in juices for a tender, flaky fillet. Prepare to be shocked at how easy this is! Pair with Peanutty Sesame Noodles (page 91) for a fabulous and fuss-free dinner party menu.

4 (6-oz) salmon fillets, preferably Wild Alaskan Salmon

½ cup Soyaki or Veri Veri Teriyaki

1 Tbsp Dijon mustard

2 green onions, chopped

1 Preheat oven broiler on high setting. Position rack on 2nd rung from the top, about 6 inches from heat.

2 Combine Soyaki and mustard. Pour over salmon and let it marinate for 10 minutes while oven is heating.

3 Place seasoned fillets on a foil-lined baking sheet, skin side down. Discard used marinade. Broil salmon for 6 minutes or until fish flakes easily.

4 Top with green onions.

Note: If you prefer to cook the fish on the stove, heat a grill pan over medium heat. Cook 2-3 minutes on each side.

Prep time: *5 minutes,* **Hands-off cooking time:** *6 minutes,* Serves 4

Per serving: 329 calories, 17 g fat, 3 g saturated fat, 37 g protein, 4 g carbs, 0 g fiber, 3 g sugar, 433 mg sodium

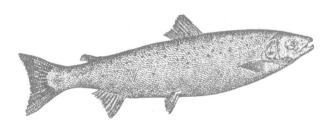

Gyoza Salad

Trader Joe's Gyoza Potstickers are delicious, inexpensive, and versatile. In addition to serving them alone as appetizers, we also use them in soups. Here we stir-fry them with vegetables in a salad. Don't microwave these beauties – pan-fry them until they are lightly browned, and then add water to steam them for a few minutes. Use any combination of crunchy vegetables, including bell peppers, onions, broccoli, or asparagus.

1 (16-oz) bag frozen gyoza or potstickers

1 ½ cups sliced carrots

1 ½ cups sugar snap peas

¼ cup Sesame Soy Ginger Vinaigrette (more if you prefer a heavier sauce)

1 Cook gyoza according to package directions. We strongly recommend pan-frying instead of microwaving. If you choose to pan-fry, toss vegetables in with the water and steam with the gyoza. Otherwise, steam or pan-fry vegetables separately until tender-crisp.

2 Pour dressing over gyoza and vegetables. Stir until coated.

Prep and cooking time: *15 minutes,* **Serves** *4*

Per serving: 229 calories, 3 g fat, 1 g saturated fat, 11 g protein, 39 g carbs, 4 g fiber, 9 g sugar, 628 mg sodium

* Use vegetarian gyoza

Saag Paneer Lasagna

This dish is fusion cooking at its most eclectic. Most people might not pair Indian and Italian cooking, but the combination of spinach and ricotta is the crossover reminiscent of Saag Paneer and spinach lasagna. This tasty twist on two classics is delicious without being heavy.

1 (16-oz) pkg "no boil" lasagna noodles

2 (15-oz) jars Masala Simmer Sauce

1 (16-oz) bag frozen chopped spinach

1 cup frozen peas, thawed

1 (15-oz) container ricotta cheese

1 (16-oz) bag shredded mozzarella cheese

1 Preheat oven to 375º F.

2 Spray or wipe a 9 x 13–inch baking pan with olive oil. Spread a few Tbsp sauce on the bottom. Add a single layer of lasagna noodles.

3 Thaw spinach, or place it in a colander under cool water until thawed. Drain well, squeezing out excess water with your hands.

4 In a bowl, combine spinach, peas, and remaining sauce. Mix well.

5 Layer ¼ of spinach mixture over noodles, followed by ⅓ of the ricotta and another layer of noodles. Press down lightly to compact layers. Repeat layering 2 more times. Spread final ¼ of spinach mixture on noodles and top with mozzarella.

6 Cover loosely with foil and bake for 25 minutes. Remove foil and cook 20 minutes longer, allowing cheese to get bubbly and golden.

Prep time: *10 minutes,*
Hands-off cooking time: *45 minutes,* **Serves 8**

Per serving: 498 calories, 19 g fat, 9 g saturated fat, 33 g protein, 55 g carbs, 5 g fiber, 14 g sugar, 908 mg sodium

Turkey BLT Sandwich

The BLT (bacon, lettuce, and tomato) is the 2nd most popular sandwich in the U.S. We dialed up the flavors by using herb focaccia bread, and a splash of balsamic vinegar to add some tang and sweetness. If you're nervous about trying balsamic vinegar on a sandwich, try adding a little mustard. It adds a nice dimension to the traditional BLT, which uses just mayonnaise. If using regular sandwich bread, try adding slices of basil for fresh herbal aroma.

For each sandwich:

1 piece Herb Focaccia bread bread, cut in half horizontally, or 2 slices bread of your choice

3 slices turkey bacon, or bacon of your choice (Trader Joe's has many uncured varieties)

Lettuce leaves

3-4 slices tomato

½ tsp balsamic vinegar

1 Tbsp mayonnaise

1 Cook bacon according to package instructions. Toast bread, if desired.

2 Spread vinegar on one of the slices of bread. Then spread mayonnaise on both slices.

3 Assemble sandwich by layering the bacon, lettuce, and tomato between bread slices.

Prep and cooking time: *5-10 minutes,* **Makes** *1 sandwich*

Per sandwich: 292 calories, 11 g fat, 1 g saturated fat, 24 g protein, 32 g carbs, 2 g fiber, 5 g sugar, 878 mg sodium

* Use vegetarian bacon

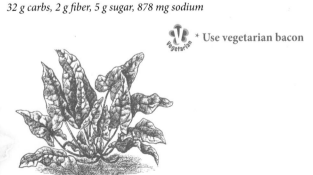

Mini-Meatloaves

We love making mini-meatloaves using muffin or cupcake tins. This meatloaf is a new twist on an old classic. We like making them with lean turkey, but you could use beef for a more traditional meatloaf. Kids love it when we serve these at parties.

1 (~1.3 lb) pkg ground turkey or ground beef

1 medium yellow onion, finely chopped

1 russet potato, boiled and mashed

1 Tbsp olive oil

½ cup quick cooking rolled oats

2 cloves garlic, crushed, or 2 cubes frozen Crushed Garlic

1 egg, lightly beaten

½ cup barbecue sauce

To brush on top:

¼ cup ketchup

¼ cup barbecue sauce

1 Preheat oven to 350º F.

2 Oil cupcake/muffin tins or spray well with non-stick cooking spray.

3 Sauté onion in olive oil until soft. Cool. In a large bowl, combine onion and remaining ingredients. Mix thoroughly.

4 Fill muffin tins with meat mixture, using ½ cup for each "muffin." Using your fingers, shape each one into a mounded muffin shape.

5 Combine ketchup and barbecue sauce and brush tops of muffins.

6 Bake for 30 minutes. (If you have a meat thermometer, they are done when the center measures 170º F). When they're done, run a knife along the edge of each muffin and pop them out of the tin

Prep time: *10 minutes*
Hands-off cooking time: *30 minutes*
Makes *8 mini-meatloaves*

Per mini-meatloaf: 226 calories, 3 g fat,
1 g saturated fat, 20 g protein, 27 g carbs,
2 g fiber, 10 g sugar, 394 mg sodium

* **Use GF oats**

Vegetable Tikka Masala

Vegetarian or Chicken Tikka Masala is one of our favorite Indian dishes. When you add yogurt to Masala sauce, you get a Tikka Masala sauce that is nicely balanced with the cooling taste of yogurt, complex and very creamy, but not at all heavy.   It is great over plain steamed basmati rice or quinoa, along with some Tandoori Naan (available fresh or frozen in several flavors).

1 (15-oz) jar Masala Simmer Sauce

1 (12-oz) bag cauliflower florets (3 cups bite-size cauliflower florets)

1 medium zucchini, unpeeled, diced into ½ inch chunks (about 1 cup)

½ cup frozen peas

¾ cup canned garbanzo beans

½ cup thinly sliced carrots (optional)

½ cup plain yogurt, such as Plain Cream Line Yogurt

1   Pour masala sauce in a wide large saucepan over medium heat.

2   Add cauliflower, zucchini, peas, garbanzo beans, and carrots. Stir until all ingredients are coated.

3   Once simmering, cover pan and turn heat to medium-low. Simmer for an additional 12-15 minutes or until cauliflower and carrots are just tender.

4   Take out 1 cup of the curry mix and stir in yogurt to temper it (so that the yogurt won't curdle). Stir this back into the pan, bring to a simmer again, and then remove from heat.

Prep time: *5 minutes,* **Hands-off cooking time:** *15-20 minutes,* **Serves** *4*

Per serving: 175 calories, 5 g fat, 1 g saturated fat, 9 g protein, 27 g carbs, 7 g fiber, 14 g sugar, 592 mg sodium

Stir-Fried Pasta with Sun Dried Tomatoes

When Deana was in graduate school, her housemate Tom would make a dish very similar to this pasta. Tom was a good cook and also the only male grad student she'd ever met who had a subscription to *Bon Appétit* magazine. The ingredients in this dish are simple, but they come together with a fabulous toasty flavor from the light stir-frying of the pasta.

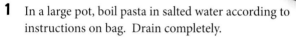

1 (16-oz) bag fusilli pasta

1 (8.5-oz) jar Julienne Sliced Sun Dried Tomatoes

½ cup packed finely chopped Italian parsley

⅔ cup toasted pine nuts

¾ cup shredded Parmesan cheese

1 In a large pot, boil pasta in salted water according to instructions on bag. Drain completely.

2 Drain jar of sun dried tomatoes and reserve drained oil (nearly ½ cup!). In the same large pot as before, heat 4 Tbsp of this oil over high heat. Add pasta and stir with a spatula or spoon. Stir-fry pasta for a couple minutes, stirring to keep pasta moving around. Don't worry if pasta starch sticks to the bottom and browns/toasts.

3 Remove pasta from heat and add sun dried tomatoes, parsley, pine nuts, and Parmesan. Toss together and serve.

Note: Don't fret about the pot being hard to clean. Any pasta starch stuck to the bottom of the pan will wash right out after 5-10 minutes of soaking. Really! Use the remaining reserved oil to sauté veggies or add to another dish.

Prep time and cooking time: *15-20 minutes,* Serves *8*

Per serving: 436 calories, 20 g fat, 4 g saturated fat, 12 g protein, 57 g carbs, 4 g fiber, 8 g sugar, 221 mg sodium

* Use brown rice pasta

Okey-Gnocchi with Pancetta & Peas

Gnocchi, Italian for "lumps" or "knots," are tender bite-size lumps of potato-based dough. Their distinctive shape, with ridges on one side like a seashell, gives the sauce a surface to cling onto. Trader Joe's frozen gnocchi, with creamy Gorgonzola cheese sauce pieces right in the ready-to-cook package, is scrumptious on its own. Adding pancetta and peas makes it even better.

1 (16-oz) bag frozen Gnocchi Alla Gorgonzola

2 oz Pancetta mini-cubes, about half the pkg, or ½ cup chopped ham

½ cup frozen peas or 1 cup frozen chopped spinach

1 Tbsp chopped fresh basil or 1 cube frozen Chopped Basil (optional)

1   Cook pancetta over medium-high heat until browned. Place on a paper towel to drain grease.

2   Pour entire package of gnocchi in a medium saucepan and cook for 5 minutes until cheese is almost melted. Add pancetta and frozen peas; continue cooking for 3 minutes longer.

3   Stir in basil.

Prep and cooking time: *10 minutes,* **Serves 4**

Per serving: 293 calories, 15 g fat, 9 g saturated fat, 11 g protein, 27 g carbs, 2 g fiber, 5 g sugar, 717 mg sodium

Turkey Artichoke Wrap

Wraps are a versatile food. These cleverly packaged sandwiches are portable, easy to make, and really draw attention to the fillings rather than the bread. The nice thing about preparing them is that the ingredient amounts are flexible—really no need to measure. We encourage you to experiment with your own custom versions! This classic turkey and Swiss combo takes on a flavorful twist by sharing the stage with red pepper and artichoke dip. This wrap is a quick and dependable standby for lunch or a picnic. Serve with gourmet chips or fresh fruit.

Lavash Bread or a large (burrito size) flour tortilla

2 slices turkey deli meat

2 slices Swiss cheese

1 Tbsp refrigerated Grilled Artichoke & Parmesan Dip

Small handful of Organics Spring Mix

1 piece Fire Roasted Red Pepper

1 Spread artichoke dip on on one half of the tortilla, avoiding edges. Place turkey and Swiss cheese slices on the same half of the tortilla. Add red pepper and greens to the center.

2 Roll tightly.

Prep time: *5 minutes,* **Serves** *1*

Per serving: 548 calories, 21 g fat, 11 g saturated fat, 37 g protein, 47 g carbs, 3 g fiber, 2 g sugar, 1035 mg sodium

G Gluten Free

* Use brown rice tortilla

Honey Mustard Chicken

This chicken is smothered in a familiar flavor that kids and adults love. Sweet honey and tangy mustard meld in the oven to create a delicious glaze and dipping sauce. For best results, we recommend using fresh herbs. Serve with brown rice or mashed potatoes.

4 chicken breasts or 6 thighs, bone-in or boneless, skin-on or skinless

2 Tbsp olive oil

¼ cup flour

¼ tsp salt

⅛ tsp black pepper

½ cup honey

½ cup Dijon mustard

2 Tbsp fresh basil, chopped

1 Preheat oven to 375° F.

2 Heat oil in a large sauté pan over medium-high heat. Mix flour with salt and pepper. Coat chicken pieces with seasoned flour, shaking off excess. Brown chicken on all sides. Transfer to a baking dish.

3 Mix honey, mustard, and basil. Pour sauce over chicken and bake for 30 minutes. Midway through the cooking, turn and baste chicken pieces once.

Substitutions: If you can get tarragon, substitute it for the basil. Called "King of Herbs" by the French, tarragon imparts a subtle licorice flavor that goes perfectly with honey and mustard.

Prep time: *10 minutes*
Hands-off cooking time: *30 minutes,* **Serves 8**

Per serving (½ breast): 239 calories, 6 g fat, 1 g saturated fat, 25 g protein, 21 g carbs, 0 g fiber, 16 g sugar, 358 mg sodium

Pizza Bianca with Prosciutto and Asparagus

In Rome, traditional pizza Bianca or "white pizza" is made with a simple selection of mozzarella cheese, olive oil, and herbs. It is often eaten for breakfast. We've added colorful toppings to make a heartier pizza that's great any time of day. You won't miss the tomato sauce in this flavor-packed white pizza.

1 (1-lb) bag refrigerated Ready to Bake Pizza Dough or Garlic & Herb Dough

1 tsp extra virgin olive oil

1 cup Quattro Formaggio shredded cheese

4 slices prosciutto, cut into 2- or 3-inch pieces

½ cup fresh or frozen asparagus spears, thawed, and cut diagonally into 3-inch pieces

2 Tbsp shaved Parmigiano Reggiano (Parmesan) cheese

¼ cup toasted pine nuts

¼ tsp black pepper

1 Preheat oven to 500° F, preferably with a pizza stone inside.

2 Roll dough into a 10-inch circle on a lightly floured surface. Drizzle oil and rub evenly all over dough.

3 Sprinkle shredded cheese onto dough. Arrange prosciutto and asparagus pieces evenly over dough. Top with Parmesan cheese, pine nuts, and black pepper.

4 Transfer to pizza stone or baking sheet. Bake for 10 minutes or until crust is golden. Let sit for 5 minutes before serving.

Variation: Try using arugula instead of asparagus and cooked pancetta instead of prosciutto.

Prep time: *15 minutes*
Hands-off cooking time: *10 minutes,* **Serves** *4*

Per serving: 485 calories, 19 g fat, 7 g saturated fat, 24 g protein, 56 g carbs, 3 g fiber, 1 g sugar, 813 mg sodium

Egg Salad Olovieh
(Persian Egg Salad)

Salad Olovieh is a Persian (also Russian) chicken/egg/
potato salad, with pickles, peas, olives, olive oil, mayonnaise,
and lemon. As far as egg salad or chicken salad goes, it's
simply the best around. It's a great dish to make for large
gatherings and goes over well with kids.

12 eggs

4 large Russet potatoes (about 4 cups total after cooked)

2 cups shredded poached chicken or Just Chicken (or cook
your own, page 98) (optional)

2 cups frozen peas

1 cup chopped dill pickles

½ cup sliced kalamata or black olives

¾ cup mayonnaise

3 Tbsp extra virgin olive oil

2 Tbsp fresh lemon juice

Salt and pepper to taste

1 Boil potatoes (unpeeled) in a pot of water with
the water 1 inch above top of potatoes. Boil for 45
minutes or until potatoes are soft when poked with a
knife. Drain. Boiled potatoes peel very easily – just
use your fingers to slip skin off.

2 While potatoes are cooking, boil eggs. Fill pot with
cold water, add eggs gently, and place over high heat.
When water comes to a boil, remove pot from heat,
cover, and let it sit for 15 minutes. Drain, run under
cold water, and peel.

3 Mash potatoes in a large bowl (coarsely, don't try to get
it very smooth), and add frozen peas while potatoes
are still hot. The heat will thaw the peas.

4 Roughly chop eggs. To the potatoes, add eggs,
chicken, pickles, and olives and combine.

5   Add mayo, olive oil, and lemon juice to the mixture, stirring until mayo is evenly distributed throughout. Add salt and pepper to taste.

6   Chill in fridge and serve with pita pockets, baguette pieces, or other favorite sandwich bread.

Tip: What makes some hardboiled eggs easy to peel when other times you need a hammer and chisel? For eggs that peel easily, let them stay in your fridge for 4 or 5 days first before hardboiling. Very fresh eggs are hard to peel when hardboiled.

Prep time: *About 45 minutes of boiling (eggs and potatoes), but only 10 minutes of prep time after that,* **Serves 12**

Per serving: 326 calories, 16 g fat, 3 g saturated fat, 17 g protein, 30 g carbs, 3 g fiber, 4 g sugar, 384 mg sodium

* Omit chicken

Nutty Wild Rice Salad

Wild rice has a wonderful nutty flavor and hearty texture making it perfect for salads, stuffings, pilaf, and soups. On the downside, it takes a long time to cook. The good news is that Trader Joe's has fully cooked Wild Rice. This entree salad offers a symphony of textures in this dish- chewiness of wild rice, sweet burst of grapes, crunch of cashews and water chestnuts, and crisp bite of green onion.

1 (16-oz) pkg fully cooked Wild Rice

2 cups pre-cooked Just Chicken (or cook your own, pg. 98)

1 ½ cups red grapes, halved

1 cup roasted cashews, whole or pieces

1 (8-oz) can sliced water chestnuts

2-3 stems green onion, chopped

Dressing:

2 Tbsp extra virgin olive oil (for a creamier dressing, substitute 1 Tbsp mayonnaise for 1 Tbsp of oil)

1 Tbsp lemon juice

1 Open package of wild rice and put contents into a large bowl, breaking up rice. Cover and microwave for 1 minute. Cool.

2 Add chicken, grapes, cashews, water chestnuts, and green onion. Stir to combine.

3 In a small bowl, whisk together olive oil and lemon juice. Pour over salad and stir to distribute evenly.

Prep time: *10 minutes,* Serves 4

*Per serving: 559 calories, 27 g fat,
5 g saturated fat, 31 g protein, 57 g carbs,
5 g fiber, 12 g sugar, 60 mg sodium*

* Omit chicken or use
Chicken-less Strips

Shrimp Mango Salad

Shrimp and langostino tails are dressed in a light citrus dressing in this colorful salad. The burst of mango flavors and creamy avocado textures jazz up this healthy version of the classic shrimp salad.

½ lb frozen medium tail-off cooked shrimp, thawed

½ lb frozen cooked langostino tails, thawed (or 1 lb cooked shrimp, total)

2 cups mango chunks

3 oz baby spinach (half a bag)

1 ripe avocado, diced

½ cup chopped cilantro

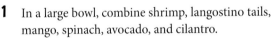

Dressing:

3 Tbsp olive oil

3 Tbsp lemon juice

3 Tbsp lime juice

1 Tbsp agave nectar or honey

½ tsp each salt and pepper

1 In a large bowl, combine shrimp, langostino tails, mango, spinach, avocado, and cilantro.

2 Whisk together ingredients for dressing. Pour over salad and gently toss to combine. Serve chilled.

Prep time: *10 minutes*, **Serves** *4*

Per serving: 352 calories, 19 g fat, 3 g saturated fat, 24 g protein, 23 g carbs, 5 g fiber, 12 g sugar, 475 mg sodium

Summer Squash Strata

A strata is similar to a frittata or quiche, but with less egg and with a thick bread layer instead of a thin crust. It's a nice breakfast or brunch dish. The assembly is easy and you can even do it the night before -- just stick it in the refrigerator overnight and pop it in the oven the next morning. This version celebrates the flavors of summer with vegetables that are in season. Play around with the ingredients. Substitute mushrooms and spinach or broccoli florets for the vegetables, use Swiss or Parmesan instead of goat cheese, or add slices of your favorite sausage.

3 medium zucchini or yellow crookneck squash, sliced into thin disks

1 (1-lb) loaf challah, cut 1-inch cubes or torn into small chunks

1 (8-oz) log goat cheese, broken into small chunks, or use Trader Joe's Crumbled Goat Cheese

2 Tbsp extra virgin olive oil, divided

1 medium yellow onion, cut in half and sliced thinly

⅓ cup jarred Julienne Sliced Sun Dried Tomatoes

2 cups whole milk

6 large eggs

½ tsp salt

¼ tsp ground black pepper

½ cup chopped fresh basil

1 Spread bread cubes in oiled 9x13-inch baking dish. Scatter half the goat cheese over bread.

2 In a skillet over medium heat, sauté onion in 1 Tbsp oil until soft, about 4-5 minutes.

3 Add squash and drizzle with 1 Tbsp oil, sautéing for an additional minute.

4 Spread vegetables on the bread layer, scattering sun dried tomatoes and remaining goat cheese over the top.

5 Whisk together milk, eggs, salt, and pepper. Pour mixture evenly over top of ingredients in baking dish. Press down gently just a little, allowing bread to soak up mixture.

6 Let dish sit 10 minutes while you preheat oven to 350° F.

7 Bake uncovered for 40-45 minutes. You will know when it's done because it will puff up quite a bit. Remove and let rest for 5-10 minutes (it will deflate back down). Sprinkle with fresh basil and serve.

Prep time: *15 minutes, plus 10 minutes for dish to sit and soak*
Hands-off cooking time: *40-45 minutes,* **Serves** 8

Per serving: 407 calories, 21 g fat, 7 g saturated fat, 17 g protein, 42 g carbs, 4 g fiber, 11 g sugar, 647 mg sodium

Gnutmeg Gnocchi with Spinach

Gnocchi are little potato dumplings that cook up in minutes, welcoming the addition of any combination of vegetables, cheeses, meats, or sauces. We love the subtle, wonderful flavor of nutmeg in this dish. Don't overdo it though — too much nutmeg can taste medicinal and bitter. Olive oil and milk create creaminess without the use of a heavy cream sauce. Spinach adds color and fresh flavor.

1 (17.6-oz) pkg dried gnocchi

1 medium yellow onion, thinly sliced

3 Tbsp extra virgin olive oil, divided

1 tsp crushed garlic or 1 cube frozen Crushed Garlic

¼ tsp nutmeg

⅛ tsp salt

½ cup roughly chopped walnuts (unsalted, raw or roasted)

¼ cup whole milk

1 (6-oz) bag fresh spinach (about 5-6 cups)

½ cup Parmesan cheese (shaved, shredded, or grated)

1 Cook gnocchi according to package directions.

2 In a deep skillet or wide saucepan, sauté onions in 2 Tbsp of olive oil until soft, about 5 minutes. Add garlic, nutmeg, salt, and walnuts, sautéing over low heat until onions begin to caramelize.

3 Add drained gnocchi to onion mixture and stir gently to combine. Drizzle another Tbsp of olive oil over gnocchi and add milk. Heat for an additional minute.

4 Place spinach on top, cover with a lid, and remove pan from heat. After a few minutes, once spinach has wilted down, add Parmesan and stir to combine.

Prep and cooking time: *15 minutes*, Serves 4

Per serving: 470 calories, 25 g fat, 6 g saturated fat,
14 g protein, 52 g carbs, 6 g fiber, 6 g sugar, 921 mg sodium

Peanutty Sesame Noodles

These are the fresh and tasty sesame peanut noodles you remember from your favorite Chinese restaurant. Serve these flavorful noodles at room temperature or cold right out of the fridge. Add cooked chicken or tofu chunks to make it a standalone one-dish meal. Or pair with Soyaki Broiled Salmon (page 72).

8 oz (half a pkg) spaghetti noodles

1 cup shredded carrot, available pre-shredded in the produce section

½ cup peeled and sliced cucumber

2 green onions, chopped

¼ cup roasted peanuts, crushed

1 Cook noodles according to package directions. Drain.

2 Pour Easy Peanutty Sauce (recipe below) over noodles and toss until noodles are evenly coated. Add carrots and cucumber. Toss gently.

3 Top with green onions and crushed peanuts.

Easy Peanutty Sauce:

¼ cup Soyaki or Veri Veri Teriyaki

¼ cup peanut butter

2 Tbsp toasted sesame oil

¼ cup water

1 Whisk Soyaki, peanut butter, and sesame oil until blended.

2 Add water and mix well.

Prep time: *10 minutes*
Hands-off cooking time: *10 minutes,* **Serves 4**

Per serving: 463 calories, 22 g fat, 3 g saturated fat, 15 g protein, 55 g carbs, 8 g fiber, 9 g sugar, 526 mg sodium

Creamy Lemony Linguine

Linguine, flavored with mushrooms and a zingy lemon pepper cream sauce, is a nice side dish for chicken or meat, or can even be a main entrée in itself. Serve with a green salad or Caesar salad.

1 (16-oz) pkg linguine pasta

1 cup heavy cream or whipping cream

½ cup shredded Parmesan cheese

Juice of 1 lemon (2 Tbsp)

2 tsp Lemon Pepper (in a grinder container)

2 Tbsp butter, unsalted

1 (10-oz) container sliced white mushrooms

1 Prepare linguine according to package instructions.

2 While linguine cooks, prepare sauce. In a small saucepan over medium heat, pour in heavy cream and add Parmesan, stirring until Parmesan is melted into the cream. Stir in lemon juice and Lemon Pepper. Turn heat to lowest setting while you prepare mushrooms.

3 In a hot skillet, melt butter and add mushrooms. Cook for 1 minute, stirring constantly, and take off heat before mushrooms give off any water. You want to keep mushrooms plump and firm, not stewed and shrunken.

4 Drain pasta when done and place in a large bowl. Pour sauce over pasta, add mushrooms, and toss together until sauce is evenly distributed.

5 Top with more Parmesan and serve.

Prep and cooking time: *15-20 minutes,* Serves *8*

Per serving: 370 calories, 16 g fat, 10 g saturated fat, 12 g protein, 46 g carbs, 3 g fiber, 4 g sugar, 153 mg sodium

* Use brown rice pasta

Pasta alla Checca

This style of pasta is a favorite all over Italy in the summer, when tomatoes and basil are at their peak. You don't have to cook a thing except for the pasta. Lovers of fresh sauces on pasta, rejoice! The mozzarella cheese will soften slightly with the heat of the pasta, making for chewy cheese balls dotted throughout the pasta.

8 oz (half a pkg) linguine pasta

1 (8-oz) container refrigerated Fresh Bruschetta Sauce

¼ cup grated Parmesan cheese

1 (8-oz) container Ciliegine, Fresh Mozzarella balls

¼ cup chopped basil

1 Cook pasta according to package directions. Drain.

2 Add bruschetta and Parmesan cheese. Mix well to coat pasta evenly.

3 Stir in mozzarella balls gently, being careful not to break them. Top with basil and serve immediately.

Prep time: *5 minutes,* **Hands-off cooking time:** *10 minutes,* Serves 4

Per serving: 421 calories, 19 g fat, 7 g saturated fat, 22 g protein, 46 g carbs, 2 g fiber, 7 g sugar, 430 mg sodium

Gluten Free   Vegetarian

* **Use brown rice pasta**

Salmon in Puff Pastry

Salmon in puff pastry, known by the fancy name Salmon En Croute, is a great dish for any special occasion. Anything is upscale when wrapped in elegant puff pastry. When you want to impress, assemble these in advance and keep in the fridge until show time.

2 lb salmon, skin removed

2 sheets frozen puff pastry, thawed but still cold

½ cup jarred Pesto Alla Genovese

½ cup roasted bell peppers, drained and sliced into strips

1 egg, beaten with a splash of water

1 Preheat oven to 375° F.

2 Spread ¼ cup pesto on half of each sheet of puff pastry, leaving a thin border on the edges for closing pastry after it's filled. Divide salmon between both sheets, cutting salmon as necessary. Top with slices of roasted peppers.

3 Brush egg white onto edges of each puff pastry sheet. Fold pastry sheets in half, closing them and pinching down on edges to seal. Cut 2-3 small slits in each pastry to let steam escape. Brush more egg wash on tops of pastry sheets.

4 Place stuffed pastry sheets on greased baking sheets and bake for 20-25 minutes, until puff pastry is golden brown and salmon is cooked. Each pastry serves 4.

Prep time: *10 minutes*
Hands-off cooking time: *20-25 minutes,* **Serves 8**

Per serving: 548 calories, 36 g fat, 15 g saturated fat, 26 g protein, 28 g carbs, 0 g fiber, 4 g sugar, 553 mg sodium

Shrimp Scampi

This dish is one of those impressive-looking meals you can truly make in a few minutes. Toss pasta into boiling water, and by the time the pasta is done, the shrimp will be ready for assembly. Simple, elegant, and easy. It's traditionally made with white wine, vermouth, or other alcohol, but we like to use fresh lemon juice instead. Lemon cuts some of the garlic and butter, giving the scampi a light, fresh flavor.

1 lb uncooked shrimp, thawed if using frozen

8 oz Spinach & Chive Linguine, or plain linguine pasta

2 Tbsp olive oil

2 Tbsp butter

3 cloves garlic, crushed, or 3 cubes frozen Crushed Garlic

½ tsp salt

¼ tsp black pepper

Pinch of red pepper flakes (optional)

¼ cup freshly squeezed lemon juice

¼ cup chopped fresh parsley

1 Cook linguine according to package directions.

2 Heat olive oil and butter in a skillet over medium-high heat. Add garlic and cook for 1 minute, being careful not to burn it. Add shrimp, salt, black pepper, and red pepper flakes; cook for 4-5 minutes, stirring frequently, until shrimp is pink and opaque. Do not overcook.

3 Remove from heat. Add lemon juice and stir until combined. Pour shrimp over drained pasta and toss lightly. Sprinkle with parsley and serve immediately.

Prep and cooking time: *15 minutes,* Serves 4

Per serving: 223 calories, 8 g fat, 2 g saturated fat, 15 g protein, 24 g carbs, 1 g fiber, 2 g sugar, 231 mg sodium

* Use brown rice pasta

Beef Stew

Stews are a true comfort food around the globe. A stew is vegetables or meats slow-cooked in liquid and served in the resulting gravy. The slow cook method allows you to use inexpensive cuts of meat that would otherwise be tough. After just a few prep steps, you can leave the stew unattended while it simmers and fills the kitchen with aromas. Traditional beef stew is made with potatoes and carrots, and we added green beans for color. Serve with biscuits or crusty bread to mop up the wonderful gravy.

1 (~1.5 lb) pkg beef stew meat, or beef chuck cut into cubes

¼ cup flour

2 Tbsp olive oil

1 (14.5-oz) can diced tomatoes

1 cup beef broth

¼ cup red wine

2 tsp Steak Sauce

2 cloves garlic, crushed, or 2 cubes frozen Crushed Garlic

2 bay leaves

3 sprigs fresh thyme, or 2 tsp dried thyme

1 lb small potatoes, cut into 1-inch chunks

2 carrots, cut into 1-inch chunks

1 small onion, cut into 1-inch chunks

2 cups green beans, cut into 1-inch pieces (optional)

¼ cup chopped parsley (optional)

1 Heat oil in large pot over medium-high heat. Dredge meat in flour, shaking off excess. Sear meat in hot oil until browned, about 1 minute per side. Browning meat seals in juices, resulting in more tender pieces. Don't overcrowd the pot, or you'll end up steaming rather than browning the meat. Cook in 2-3 batches.

2 Return seared meat to pot. Add remaining ingredients (except green beans and parsley) and stir. When liquid is boiling, reduce heat to low, cover, and simmer for 2 hours.

3 Add green beans during the last 15 minutes of cooking to preserve crispness. For softer green beans, add during the last 30 minutes of cooking.

4 Remove from heat and remove bay leaves and thyme sprigs. Sprinkle on fresh parsley right before serving.

Prep time: *15 minutes,* **Hands-off cooking time:** *2 hours,* **Serves** *6*

Per serving: 298 calories, 9 g fat, 3 g saturated fat, 26 g protein, 25 g carbs, 4 g fiber, 8 g sugar, 510 mg sodium

Your Own Just Chicken

Use this basic recipe to sauté whole juicy chicken breasts, or dice it up for use in recipes calling for pre-cooked chicken. Trader Joe's pre-cooked Just Chicken is always handy but it's simple to make your own. For an easy and very healthy dinner, serve with steamed vegetables, pasta, quinoa, or rice.

....

2 boneless, skinless chicken breasts

2 Tbsp olive oil, divided

¼ tsp salt

¼ tsp pepper

....

1 Coat breasts with 1 Tbsp oil and season with salt and pepper.

2 In a skillet, add 1 Tbsp oil and add chicken, sautéing 2 minutes each side for a golden color.

3 Reduce heat, cover, and continue to cook until chicken plumps and is cooked through (about 10 minutes)

4 Let rest for 1-2 minutes before serving.

Note: If using in a cold dish or cutting into bite-size pieces, cool first.

Prep and cooking time: *15 minutes*
Makes about *2 ½ - 3 cups cooked diced chicken*

Per serving (½ breast): 180 calories, 9 g fat,
1 g saturated fat, 25 g protein, 0 g carbs, 0 g fiber,
0 g sugar, 205 mg sodium

Simple Sides

Black Bean Cornbread

Trader Joe's Cornbread Mix is a sweet cornbread, which may come as a surprise to Southerners who enjoy a salty cornbread. Here we have created a delicious sweet and savory version by adding a can of Organic Black Bean Soup. The cornbread becomes heartier with black bean flavorings and bits of corn, onion, and tomato hidden inside. It's perfect for enjoying alongside a simple soup or chowder. Trader Joe's has a great selection of ready-to-go boxed soups. Now, here's the bonus: each piece of cornbread has only ½ gram of fat and over 5 grams of protein.

1 box Cornbread Mix

2 egg whites

1 (14.5-oz) can Organic Black Bean Soup

½ cup 2% or whole milk

1 Preheat oven to 350° F.

2 Beat together egg whites, soup, and milk.

3 Stir in dry cornbread mix. Don't add any of the other ingredients called for on box instructions.

4 Pour into oiled 8 x 8 x 2-inch baking pan and bake for 35-40 minutes or until a toothpick inserted in cornbread comes out clean.

Prep time: *5 minutes,* **Hands-off cooking time:** *35-40 minutes,* **Serves 9**

Per piece: 202 calories, 0.5 g fat, 0 g saturated fat, 5 g protein, 43 g carbs, 2 g fiber, 17 g sugar, 338 mg sodium

Coconut Curried Vegetables

Coconut milk simmers down to a creamy sauce for the vegetables in this dish. You can substitute other vegetables, such as cauliflower, green beans, or peas. Serve with Tandoori Chicken (page 47) or any other Indian or Southeast Asian entrée.

....

3 zucchini, sliced into ½-inch or 1-inch pieces

2 carrots, chopped or cut lengthwise into thin pieces

1 red bell pepper, cut into 1-inch pieces

1 cup Light Coconut Milk (half the can)

1 tsp curry powder

1 clove garlic, crushed, or 1 cube frozen Crushed Garlic

½ tsp salt

....

1 In a deep skillet or wide saucepan, combine coconut milk, curry powder, garlic, and salt.

2 Bring sauce to a simmer and add vegetables. Simmer for about 10-15 minutes until vegetables are tender.

Prep time: *5-10 minutes*
Hands-off cooking time: *10-15 minutes,* **Serves 4**

*Per serving: 82 calories, 3 g fat, 2 g saturated fat,
2 g protein, 13 g carbs, 4 g fiber, 5 g sugar,
354 mg sodium*

Broccoli Squares

This healthy dish is a cross between a quiche and a casserole, and works well as an appetizer or side dish. Ready-to-use broccoli slaw makes the preparation work a breeze. Even people that aren't crazy about green vegetables will find this savory and flavorful dish irresistible. Cut into squares for easy serving. For a tasty variation, substitute an equal amount of shredded zucchini for the broccoli.

1 (12-oz) bag Organic Broccoli Slaw, or 5 cups shredded broccoli or zucchini

4 eggs

1 Tbsp chopped fresh basil

2 Tbsp chopped fresh parsley

½ cup vegetable oil, plus 1 Tbsp

¼ tsp salt

2 cloves garlic, crushed, or 2 cubes frozen Crushed Garlic

1 cup finely chopped onion

½ cup shredded Parmesan cheese

1 cup Buttermilk Pancake and All Purpose Baking Mix (or Bisquick)

2 tsp sesame seeds (optional)

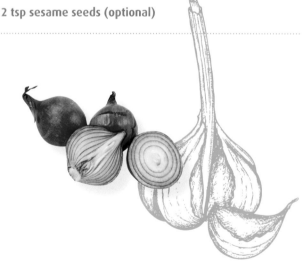

1 Preheat oven to 350° F.

2 Lightly beat eggs in a large bowl. Add herbs, ½ cup oil, salt, and garlic to the bowl and combine.

3 Sauté onions in 1 Tbsp oil until soft. Add cooked onions, Parmesan, and slaw to the bowl and mix thoroughly. Add baking mix and mix again.

4 Put mixture in an oiled oblong baking dish or an oiled 8x8-inch square baking dish, and evenly spread mixture in dish. Sprinkle with sesame seeds.

5 Bake for 35 minutes or until top is turning golden brown.

Note: You can make your own baking mix by mixing 1 cup flour, 1 Tbsp baking powder, and 1 tsp sugar; then add ¼ cup of oil and mix until it's a corn meal consistency.

Prep time: *15 minutes*
Hands-off cooking time: *35 minutes,* **Serves** *9*

Per serving: 209 calories, 16 g fat, 4 g saturated fat,
7 g protein, 10 g carbs, 1 g fiber, 3 g sugar, 290 mg sodium

Herbed Mushroom and Onion Flatbread

This beautiful yet rustic focaccia is topped with caramelized onions and hearty crimini mushrooms, which are actually baby portobellos. Experiment with whatever vegetables and toppings you have on hand.

1 (1-lb) bag Garlic & Herb Pizza Dough
½ small onion, sliced thinly
½ bag (2 cups) sliced Crimini Mushrooms
1 ½ Tbsp olive oil, divided
Pinch salt
¼ cup shredded Parmesan cheese

1 Preheat oven to 500° F (preferably with pizza stone inside).

2 On a well floured surface or on an oiled baking sheet, stretch pizza dough gently with hands to approximately a 12-inch diameter. Don't worry about rolling it perfectly flat—we're going for rustic.

3 In a skillet, sauté onion with 1 Tbsp of olive oil until onions are soft. Add mushrooms and sauté just until mushrooms are beginning to brown.

4 Top pizza dough with onions, mushrooms, and a drizzle of olive oil. Sprinkle with a little salt.

5 Place pan in oven (or transfer to the pizza stone) and bake for 15 minutes or until dough is golden.

6 Remove from oven, sprinkle with Parmesan, and serve.

Prep time: *10 minutes*
Hands-off cooking time: *15 minutes,* Serves *8*

Per serving: 172 calories, 6 g fat, 1 g saturated fat,
5 g protein, 26 g carbs, 1 g fiber, 1 g sugar, 520 mg sodium

Eggplant Zucchini Bake

This side dish uses one of our favorites at Trader Joe's, refrigerated Fresh Bruschetta Sauce. The intense flavors of the sauce play nicely against the simple combination of eggplant and zucchini. After baking, the bread crumbs get crisp, the zucchini is tender but not mushy, and the eggplant is softened and silky.

1 medium eggplant

4 medium zucchini

1 Tbsp extra virgin olive oil

1 (8-oz) container refrigerated Fresh Bruschetta Sauce

½ cup bread crumbs

1 Preheat oven to 400° F.

2 Peel and slice eggplant into (slightly thicker than) ¼-inch slices crosswise.

3 Slice zucchini lengthwise into ½-inch slices.

4 Coat bottom of an 8x12 or 9x13-inch baking pan with olive oil. Arrange eggplant slices on the bottom, and top with zucchini slices.

5 Pour bruschetta sauce evenly over the dish.

6 Sprinkle bread crumbs on top and bake for about 40 minutes.

Prep time: *10 minutes,*
Hands-off cooking time: *40 minutes*

Serves 6

Per serving: 141 calories, 8 g fat, 1 g saturated fat,
4 g protein, 18g carbs, 4 g fiber, 7 g sugar,
244 mg sodium

* Omit bread crumbs or use GF bread crumbs

Cilantro Jasmine Rice

Jasmine rice is very fragrant and delicious on its own.
We dial up the flavors with fresh cilantro. This side dish is
wonderful with our Go Go Mango Chicken (page 43) or
any Asian entrée.

1 cup uncooked jasmine rice

2 cups water

½ tsp salt

¼ cup finely chopped fresh cilantro

1   Bring water to a boil. Add salt and rice. Cover, reduce
heat to medium-low, and steam for 20 minutes or until
water is absorbed.

2   Stir in cilantro.

Prep time: *5 minutes*
Hands-off cooking time: *20 minutes*
Serves 4

Per serving: 180 calories, 1 g fat, 0 g saturated fat,
3 g protein, 40 g carbs, 1 g fiber, 0 g sugar,
291 mg sodium

Rosemary Potato Pizza

Italian friends have introduced us to fabulous specialties from Rome and Naples, including a variety of authentic pizzas. Pizza night may feature a dozen unique and different pizzas with an array of fresh vegetables and various cheeses. One of our favorites is potato pizza. Our friends make their own dough, but we can cheat a little with Trader Joe's ready made dough. Pair with a fresh salad.

1 (1-lb) bag plain pizza dough

1 russet potato, peeled and very thinly sliced

2 Tbsp extra virgin olive oil, divided

½ tsp salt

1 Tbsp packed fresh rosemary

1 Preheat oven to 525° F, preferably with a pizza stone inside. If you don't have a pizza stone, just use an oiled baking pan, which needs no preheating.

2 Drizzle potato slices with 1 Tbsp olive oil and sprinkle with salt. Let sit while you roll out dough.

3 Roll out dough thinly on a floured surface, using a rolling pin or your hands. If using a baking pan, simply fit dough to the baking pan

4 Cover surface of pizza with a single layer of potatoes. Sprinkle on rosemary and drizzle with remaining olive oil.

5 Bake pizza for about 12 minutes or until crust is golden.

Prep time: *10 minutes*
Hands-off cooking time: *12 minutes,* **Serves** *4*

Per serving (¼ pizza): 383 calories, 9 g fat,
1 g saturated fat, 11 g protein, 64 g carbs, 3 g fiber,
0 g sugar, 593 mg sodium

Olive-Stuffed Bread

A few minutes of work yields a rustic yet sophisticated crusty herbed-bread loaf with the salty surprise of olives inside. It's a nice bread to enjoy warm with cheese, alongside an appetizer, or with a full meal.

1 (1-lb) bag refrigerated dough

½ cup Green Olive Tapenade or your favorite bruschetta or tapenade

1 Preheat oven to 425° F. If using a pizza stone, make sure it is preheated in the oven.

2 On a floured surface, roll dough (or stretch out with hands) so it is about 6 x 15 inches. Spoon tapenade down the center lengthwise, except for the last inch at each end. Pull up sides of bread and firmly pinch a seam down the center, sealing in bruschetta.

3 Place on a pizza stone or an oiled baking sheet and bake for 30-35 minutes, or until crust is golden brown.

4 Slice loaf into 1-inch pieces and serve warm.

Prep time: *5 minutes,*
Hands-off cooking time: *30 minutes,* **Serves 8**

Per serving: 150 calories, 4 g fat, 0 g saturated fat,
3 g protein, 25 g carbs, 1 g fiber, 0 g sugar, 660 mg sodium

Crunchy Broccoli Slaw

This interesting twist to traditional coleslaw uses shredded broccoli instead of cabbage. The suggested dressings are all good alternatives to the traditional (and very high fat/calorie) mayonnaise dressing. For a homemade dressing, mix a 2:1 ratio of extra virgin olive oil and balsamic vinegar whisked with a little Dijon mustard.

1 (12-oz) bag Organic Broccoli Slaw, or 5 cups shredded broccoli and carrots

½ cup Tuscan Italian Vinaigrette or Sweet Poppyseed Dressing (if you like sweeter dressings)

⅓ cup sliced green onion (2 stalks)

½ cup raw sunflower seeds

½ cup slivered almonds

1 Combine dressing and slaw. Toss until evenly distributed.

2 Add remaining ingredients and combine.

3 Chill and serve.

Variation: For an Asian-inspired slaw, use Sesame Soy Ginger Vinaigrette (fat free).

Prep time: *5 minutes,* **Serves 8**

Per serving: 109 calories, 8 g fat, 1 g saturated fat, 5 g protein, 6 g carbs, 2 g fiber, 0 g sugar, 275 mg sodium

Spinach & Feta Stuffed Baby Portobellos

Portobello mushrooms have an earthy flavor and meaty texture. Trader Joe's carries smaller "stuffing portobellos" which are only 2 inches across and perfect for a filling. Stuffed mushrooms are attractive, fancy-looking, self-contained morsels. Two of these on a plate make a perfect side dish.

18 Stuffing Portobellos

2 cups frozen spinach

1 Tbsp extra virgin olive oil

½ medium yellow onion, chopped

½ cup bread crumbs

Scant ½ tsp salt

⅓ cup Crumbled Feta with Mediterranean Herbs (plain is fine too)

1 Preheat oven to 400° F (stove top instructions are also included in the steps 7-8).

2 Clean mushrooms and remove stems. Chop up stems and set aside.

3 Thaw spinach and thoroughly squeeze out all water. Don't be shy - use your hands and squeeze firmly. 2 cups of frozen spinach will turn into about ½ cup of thawed and drained spinach. Place in bowl.

4 Heat oil in skillet over medium heat and sauté onions for a minute or two. Add mushroom stems and sauté until onions are soft. Discard any juices. Add onion mixture to the bowl.

5 Add bread crumbs and salt to the bowl and combine thoroughly.

6 Gently stir in feta.

7 Stuff each mushroom cap with filling. Arrange caps, stuffing side up, on an oiled pan (for oven method) or in an oiled lidded skillet (for stove top method) or on a platter (for grilling).

8 Cook for 7-8 minutes in oven, 5 minutes in a lidded skillet over medium high heat, or a few minutes on the grill. Ovens, grills, and burners can vary, so stop cooking the second the mushrooms look heated through and tender. You want to stop cooking before they start losing water and stewing.

Prep time: *15-20 minutes,*
Hands-off cooking time: *7-8 minutes,* **Serves** 9

Per serving (2 stuffed portobellos): 90 calories, 3 g fat, 1 g saturated fat, 6 g protein, 12 g carbs, 2 g fiber, 4 g sugar, 280 mg sodium

Wilted Spinach with Attitude

It's easy to eat your spinach when it's this tasty and easy to make. As a child, Wona remembers trying to force down cafeteria-style over-cooked spinach drowning in vinegar– it's no wonder kids hated spinach back then. This version is nothing like that. Fresh spinach is cooked quickly until just wilted, preserving a vibrant green color and fresh flavor.

2 (6-oz) bags baby spinach

1 Tbsp olive oil

3 cloves garlic, crushed, or 3 cubes frozen Crushed Garlic

¼ cup water

½ tsp salt

Juice from half a lemon (optional)

1   Heat olive oil in a large pan over medium-high heat. Add garlic and fry for 30 seconds, being careful not to let the garlic brown. Garlic burns easily and tastes bitter when browned.

2   Add spinach, water, and salt. Cover and cook for 2 minutes. Lift cover and stir spinach with tongs, tossing leaves so that all the spinach wilts evenly.

3   As soon as all leaves are wilted, remove from heat. Squeeze half a lemon over spinach and mix. Serve immediately.

Prep time: *2 minutes,* **Cooking time:** *3 minutes,* **Serves** *4*

Per serving: 54 calories, 4 g fat, 1 g saturated fat, 3 g protein, 4 g carbs, 2 g fiber, 0 g sugar, 357 mg sodium

Pan-Toasted Brussels Sprouts

Who hasn't eaten a Brussels sprout and pretended to be a giant eating an entire head of cabbage in one bite? Chicken broth steams and flavors the Brussels sprouts, making them ready in a hurry in this fabulous pan-fried recipe. The Guinness record for eating Brussels sprouts is 44 in one minute. Try our recipe and you might be a contender.

1 (12-oz) pkg Brussels sprouts

2 tsp olive oil or butter

½ cup chicken broth or vegetable broth

Grated or shredded Parmesan cheese (optional)

1 Heat olive oil in saucepan over medium heat.

2 Cut Brussels sprouts in half. Place them cut-side down in hot pan. Add chicken broth. When broth comes to a boil, cover and cook for 5 minutes.

3 Remove lid and continue to cook until broth evaporates and Brussels sprouts are browned.

4 Remove from heat and sprinkle with Parmesan cheese.

Prep & cooking time: *10 minutes,* Serves *4*

Per serving: 63 calories, 3 g fat, 0 g saturated fat, 2 g protein, 6 g carbs, 3 g fiber, 2 g sugar, 97 mg sodium

* Choose GF broth

Garlic Bread

Garlic bread doesn't have to drip with butter to be delicious. Try our version, which uses a flavorful combination of olive oil and butter instead. The recipe will yield a crunchy crust, but if you prefer a softer bread, simply skip the toasting in step #5 Serve with our Classic Lasagna (page 58) or on its own as an appetizer.

....

1 loaf Italian bread

3 Tbsp butter, softened at room temperature

3 Tbsp olive oil

3 cloves garlic, crushed, or 3 cubes frozen Crushed Garlic, thawed

½ tsp salt

2 Tbsp chopped fresh basil, or 2 tsp dried basil (you could use parsley if you prefer)

½ cup mozzarella cheese (optional)

¼ cup shredded Parmesan cheese (optional)

....

1 Preheat oven to 350º F.

2 Slice loaf in half down the middle, as if you were making a sub sandwich.

3 Mix together butter, olive oil, garlic, salt, and basil. Spread evenly on both cut sides of bread. Place both halves together again and wrap with aluminum foil.

4 Bake for 15 minutes.

5 Remove from oven, remove foil, and sprinkle cheese on insides if desired. Return to oven, cut side up, for 10 minutes longer or until browned to your desire.

Prep time: *5 minutes,*
Hands-off cooking time: *15-25 minutes,* **Serves** *12*

Per serving: 203 calories, 6 g fat, 2 g saturated fat,
5 g protein, 32 g carbs, 3 g fiber, 1 g sugar, 564 mg sodium

Raita (Cucumber Yogurt Dip)

Raita is a traditional accompaniment to spicy and very flavorful Indian and Middle Eastern dishes. Cucumber, yogurt, and mint are such a refreshing and cooling combination. The raisins are a nice balance to both the taste and texture of this dish. Serve this dish as an appetizer with cut pita triangles or pita chips, or as a side dish to any Indian or Middle Eastern meal.

2 cups plain yogurt, such as Plain Cream Line Yogurt or Greek Style Plain Yogurt

½ cup raisins

1 cup peeled and finely diced cucumber

2 Tbsp finely chopped fresh mint or 2 tsp dried mint

¼ tsp salt

1 Mix all ingredients in a serving bowl and serve right away.

2 Raita can be chilled in the fridge for 1 or 2 hours if prepared ahead of time, but it doesn't keep well overnight since the raisins swell.

Prep time: *10 minutes,* Serves 6

Per serving: 97 calories, 3 g fat, 2 g saturated fat, 3 g protein, 14 g carbs, 1 g fiber, 5 g sugar, 129 mg sodium

Spinach Timbales (Crustless Spinach Mini-Quiche)

We love old cookbooks. One of our favorites is called *Who Says We Can't Cook!* published in 1955 by the Women's National Press Club. In this book, every recipe comes with a captivating description and background story. Our favorite section contains contributed recipes from celebrities and the who's who of the White House. We found Grace Coolidge's (Mrs. Calvin Coolidge) recipe for spinach timbales and decided to make an updated and healthier version. A timbale is a custard-like dish with meat or veggies made in individual round molds, a unique way to serve spinach.

....

1 (1-lb) bag frozen spinach

½ cup finely chopped onion

2 eggs

1 cup whole milk

½ tsp salt

¼ tsp black pepper

⅛ tsp nutmeg (freshly ground if you have it)

Shredded Parmesan (optional, for garnish)

....

1 Preheat oven to 350º F.

2 Thaw spinach. Thoroughly squeeze out all the water with your hands. Don't be shy—really squeeze. By the time you've squeezed out all the water, remaining spinach should measure about 1 cup packed.

3 Sauté onions in olive oil until soft and translucent.

4 Put spinach in a medium bowl. Beat eggs and add to the bowl. Add milk, onion, salt, pepper, and nutmeg. Mix well.

5 Oil 6 small ramekins (6-oz size, 3.5 inch diameter) or use cooking spray. Add ⅓ cup mixture to each ramekin and flatten tops. Place ramekins in a 9x13-inch baking dish. Fill outer tray with hot water halfway up the sides of ramekins. Be careful not to get any water inside ramekins.

6 Bake uncovered for 30 minutes.

7 Remove ramekins from hot water bath. When they are cool enough to handle, run the edge of a knife along the sides and pop timbales out onto your plate. Serve immediately.

Prep time: *15 minutes,*
Hands-off cooking time: *30 minutes,* **Serves** 6
Makes *6 timbales*

Per timbale: 74 calories, 3 g fat, 1 g saturated fat,
4 g protein, 5 g carbs, 2 g fiber, 4 g sugar,
337 mg sodium

Baked Sweet Potato Fries

Fries are irresistible, and this lean version of the deep-fried variety is also guilt-free. While not quite as crispy as classic French fries, what they lack in crispness, they make up for in flavor from using sweet potatoes. Serve with burgers, sandwiches, or entrées such as our Mini-Meatloaves (page 76). These are so popular at our house, we always double the recipe (in which case, use two baking sheets).

1 (12-oz) bag pre-cut Sweet Potato Spears

1 Tbsp olive oil

¼ tsp salt

¼ tsp curry powder or ground cumin (optional)

1 Preheat oven to 400° F.

2 Toss sweet potatoes with olive oil, until spears are evenly coated. Sprinkle with salt and curry, and mix again.

3 Spread spears in a single layer on a baking sheet. Bake for 20-30 minutes until cooked, stirring halfway through cooking for best results.

4 Serve immediately. Baked fries get soggy quickly.

Variation: For garlic fries: use 1 tsp crushed garlic or ½ tsp garlic powder instead of curry powder. Sprinkle with chopped parsley just before serving.

Prep time: *5 minutes,*
Hands-off cooking time: *20-30 minutes,* Serves 4

Per serving: 90 calories, 3 g fat, 0 g saturated fat,
1 g protein, 15 g carbs, 3 g fiber, 3 g sugar,
155 mg sodium

Sautéed Sweet Corn with Pine Nuts

This recipe from Heidi H. was inspired by a dish she had while traveling in Guangzhou, China. While the dish is simple, the flavor combination is surprising and unique. Serve this side with any Asian entrée. Eating this dish with chopsticks may prove to be a challenge, so we recommend having spoons or forks at the ready.

1 (15-oz) can corn

1 (8-oz) pkg raw pine nuts

2 Tbsp olive oil

2 Tbsp soy sauce or tamari

1 Mix olive oil and soy sauce together.

2 In a skillet or wok, heat the oil/soy sauce mixture on medium-low heat.

3 Toss pine nuts into pan and cook for 2-3 minutes, stirring frequently.

4 Add corn and fry 2 minutes longer, stirring to combine.

Prep and cooking time: *5 minutes,* **Serves 8**

Per serving: 254 calories, 23 g fat, 2 g saturated fat, 5 g protein, 9 g carbs, 2 g fiber, 5 g sugar, 215 mg sodium

* **Use tamari instead of soy sauce**

Cooking with Trader Joe's Cookbook Companion

Delicious Desserts
and
Daring Drinks

Decadent Chocolate Custard

Once you learn to appreciate dark chocolate, it's nearly impossible to go back to milk chocolate, which has more sugar and milk in it than actual chocolate. Our favorite dark chocolate at Trader Joe's is Valrhona, available in three "strengths" (percentages of cacao, 56, 71 and 82%). It's very smooth, intense, and melts beautifully. This easy chocolate custard doesn't require baking, only cooking and stirring on the stovetop.

1 cup heavy cream

2 egg yolks

1 (3.5-oz) bar dark chocolate

1 Whisk heavy cream and yolks together in a saucepan. Bring heat to medium-low and continue stirring.

2 Break chocolate into pieces and add to saucepan, continually stirring until chocolate melts completely and mixture looks very smooth and even in color. Make sure mixture never comes to a boil, otherwise it will curdle and separate.

3 Once mixture has thickened (coats a spoon thickly, about 10 minutes), remove from heat and pour into 4 small ramekins or 3-oz glass bowls.

4 Chill for about an hour. For a thicker consistency (thicker than a custard) chill for about 2-3 hours.

Prep and cooking time: *15 minutes,* **Serves** *4*

Per serving: 368 calories, 32 g fat, 21 g saturated fat, 3 g protein, 10 g carbs, 3 g fiber, 7 g sugar, 44 mg sodium

Honey Mint Fruit Salad

For a light finish to any meal, try a fruit salad made with fresh fruits in season. Choose any combination of fruits such as strawberries, blueberries, melon balls, kiwi, and grapes. Brighten up the flavors with a touch of honey, mint, and lime.

1 heaping cup of fruits in season (cut up large pieces)

1 tsp chopped mint leaves (a few leaves)

1 tsp lime juice

1 tsp honey

1 To make dressing, mix together mint leaves, honey, and lime juice.

2 Place fruits in a bowl and drizzle with dressing.

Prep time: *5-10 minutes,* **Serves** *1*

G Gluten Free   V Vegetarian

Per serving: 131 calories, 1 g fat, 0 g saturated fat,
2 g protein, 33 g carbs, 4 g fiber, 27 g sugar, 25 mg sodium

Peachy Sangria

A white version of its classic cousin, Sangria, this peachy version is light and crisp. Make it ahead of time to allow the fruity flavors to meld. This refreshing drink is great for brunch or a light dinner on the patio.

1 bottle dry white wine, such as Barefoot Pinot Grigio

½ cup Montbisou Pêches or other peach liqueur (optional)

2 Tbsp sugar

1 peach, unpeeled and cut into wedges

1 cup assorted colors grapes, halved

1 cup mineral water or club soda

1 Pour wine and peach liqueur into a glass pitcher. Add sugar and stir until dissolved. Drop in fruits. Keep in fridge at least 4 hrs or up to 3 days.

2 Just before serving, stir in mineral water.

Prep time: *10 minutes, Serves 4*

Per serving: 213 calories, 0 g fat, 0 g saturated fat, 1 g protein, 23 g carbs, 1 g fiber, 14 g sugar, 1 mg sodium

G Gluten Free **V** Vegetarian

Coconut Rice with Mango

This Southeast Asian dessert is a take on Sticky Rice with Mango, which is made with glutinous rice. Our version uses fragrant jasmine rice.

½ cup jasmine rice

½ cup water

1 cup + ¼ cup Light Coconut Milk

3 Tbsp sugar

½ cup Mango Sauce or Mango Nectar (optional)

2 cups refrigerated Fresh Cut Mango or frozen Mango Chunks, thawed

1 Combine rice, water, 1 cup coconut milk, and sugar in a saucepan. Bring mixture to a boil. Reduce heat and cover. Simmer over low heat for 30 minutes or until rice is cooked. Remove from heat and let rice sit covered for another 10 minutes.

2 Drizzle 2 Tbsp of mango sauce onto each dessert plate. Place a dollop of coconut rice on center of plate. Top rice with a spoonful of reserved coconut milk, letting it run down the sides. Top with a few slices of mango and serve.

Prep time: *10 minutes,*
Hands-off cooking time: *30 minutes,* **Serves** *4*

Per serving: 240 calories, 4 g fat, 3 g saturated fat, 2 g protein, 49 g carbs, 3 g fiber, 22 g sugar, 17 mg sodium

No Moo Mousse

This delicious chocolate mousse has rich, intense flavor from dark chocolate and creaminess from light coconut milk, not heavy cream or any other dairy products. Vegans and lactose-intolerant folks everywhere can rejoice. The extra bonus is that light coconut milk has a fraction of the calories of heavy cream, making this mousse a better choice for anyone watching their calories.

Mousse:

2 (3.5-oz) bars dark bittersweet chocolate, such as Valrhona 71% Cacao

1 (14-oz) can Light Coconut Milk

2 Tbsp Captain Morgan Original Spiced Rum (optional; do not use regular rum)

Topping:

Any selection of fresh berries or mango

1 Melt chocolate in one of two ways:

- **Microwave method:** Break up chocolate bars into squares (8 squares for each bar) and place in a small Pyrex bowl. Microwave for 1 minute and stir. Repeat with 30-second intervals, stirring after every interval until fully melted. Wait a minute between intervals to let the heat of the bowl dissipate. Melting 2 chocolate bars should take about a total of 2 minutes. Be careful not to burn the chocolate.

- **Stovetop method:** Place 3-4 cups water in a pot and bring to a boil. Place a glass Pyrex bowl on top of boiling water (bottom of bowl should not touch water) and place chocolate pieces in bowl. Steam from boiling water will gently melt chocolate without scorching it.

2 Add coconut milk and rum to blender. Pour melted chocolate into blender and blend right away for about 30 seconds. Pour mousse into individual cups or ramekins and place in fridge for two hours. If leaving them in the fridge longer than a couple of hours or making it the day before, cover mousse cups with plastic wrap.

3 If desired, top each mousse cup generously with fresh fruit right before serving

Prep time: *10 minutes. Make at least 2 hours ahead of time*
Serves *8*

*Per serving: 179 calories, 12 g fat, 8 g saturated fat,
2 g protein, 10 g carbs, 4 g fiber, 8 g sugar,
37 mg sodium*

Just Peachy Pie

Nothing says summer like fresh peach pie. If your peaches have thin peels, don't even bother peeling them. Trader Joe's frozen pie crusts are flakey, free of transfats, and easy to use. Simply thaw the crusts on the counter and then unfold them. If there are any holes, just patch them by pressing the dough together with your fingers—repairs won't be noticeable after the pie is baked.

1 box frozen pie crusts (2 crusts), thawed

2 lbs peaches, pitted and sliced (about 6 cups cut peaches)

1 Tbsp lemon juice

¼ cup all purpose flour

½ cup sugar

1 Preheat oven to 425° F.

2 Line pie plate with the first crust. In a bowl, combine peaches, lemon juice, flour, and sugar. Put filling in the pie and top with second crust, pinching crust edges together.

3 Poke top crust once or twice with the tip of a knife.

4 Bake 40-45 minutes until top is golden. If edges start to brown too much, cover them with a few strips or ring of foil.

5 Serve warm, or cool completely and serve later. Serve plain, or add some whipped cream or vanilla ice cream.

Prep time: *15 minutes,*
Hands-off cooking time: *45 minutes,* Serves *8*

Per serving: 448 calories, 24 g fat, 14 g saturated fat,
5 g protein, 51 g carbs, 2 g fiber, 22 g sugar, 420 mg sodium

Lemon Basil Cake

It might sound odd to put basil in a cake, but compare to how mint is used to flavor sweet desserts. We're used to adding spices like cinnamon and nutmeg to desserts, but herbs are not as popular. Lately, however, herbs are popping up in sweet desserts everywhere, including rosemary cake, basil sherbet, and lavender custard. Lemon and basil combine deliciously to turn ordinary vanilla cake into something unique and flavorful.

1 pkg Vanilla Cake & Baking Mix (requires 2 eggs, 1 stick melted butter or ½ cup oil, and 1 cup cold milk)

Zest of 2 lemons, about 2 Tbsp (use a lemon zester to make it easy)

½ cup finely chopped fresh basil

Blueberries or whipped cream (optional)

1 Preheat oven to 350° F.

2 Mix together cake batter as directed. When the batter is smooth, stir in lemon zest and basil.

3 Spread batter in oiled 8x8-inch pan. Bake 40-43 minutes or until toothpick inserted in center comes out clean.

4 Cool and remove from pan. When serving slices, top with blueberries or whipped cream.

Prep time: *5-10 minutes,*
Hands-off cooking time: *40 minutes,* **Serves 9**

Per serving: 312 calories, 13 g fat, 7 g saturated fat, 5 g protein, 45 g carbs, 1 g fiber, 26 g sugar, 438 mg sodium

Basic Lemonade

We love to make this basic lemonade at home, and whenever our kids set up a lemonade stand, neighbors and passersby say that it's the best they've ever tasted. We often add a splash of rose water, which takes the lemonade to an exotic level. If you use rose water, make sure it's distilled rose water, not diluted rose oil. Any Middle Eastern grocery will have good, inexpensive rose water.

1 cup water

1 cup sugar

1 cup fresh lemon juice (about 5 lemons)

5 cups water

2 cups crushed ice

2 Tbsp rose water (optional)

1 Combine 1 cup water and sugar in a saucepan over medium-low heat and stir until sugar dissolves. Remove from heat. This is your sugar syrup.

2 In a pitcher or other container, combine sugar syrup, lemon juice, 5 cups water, ice, and rose water.

3 Taste and adjust for sweetness.

Prep time: *10 minutes,* **Serves** *10*

Per serving: 83 calories, 0 g fat, 0 g saturated fat, 0 g protein, 22 g carbs, 0 g fiber, 21 g sugar, 5 mg sodium

Honey Cardamom Lemonade

Cardamom is a warm, exotic, aromatic spice with citrusy undertones that go well with lemonade. After working out, try adding a pinch of salt. The salt balances the sweet and tart flavors of lemonade and replaces electrolytes lost due to sweating. Lemonade made with fresh lemons also has the added benefit of vitamin C, potassium, antioxidants, and anticancer plant chemicals.

1 cup water

1 cup honey

1 cup fresh lemon juice (about 5 lemons)

5 cups water

2 cups crushed ice

½ tsp finely ground cardamom

1 Combine 1 cup water and the honey in a saucepan over medium-low heat and stir until honey dissolves. Remove from heat. This is your honey syrup.

2 In a pitcher or other container, combine honey syrup, lemon juice, 5 cups water, ice, and cardamom.

3 Taste and adjust for sweetness.

Tip: Store lemonade in a pitcher or recycle a well-rinsed glass juice bottle.

Prep time: *10 minutes,* **Serves** *10*

Per serving: 101 calories, 0 g fat, 0 g saturated fat, 0 g protein, 29 g carbs, 0 g fiber, 26 g sugar, 5 mg sodium

Saffron Rice Pudding

Saffron and cardamom turn ordinary rice pudding into an exotic dessert. We adapted this recipe from *New Food of Life*, a lovely cookbook of modernized Persian recipes. Make sure to use distilled rose water (found at any Middle Eastern grocer), not diluted rose oil.

1 cup rice, preferably basmati

8 cups water

1 cup sugar

2 Tbsp unsalted butter

1 tsp Spanish Saffron threads (half the jar), or ½ tsp ground saffron

1 tsp ground cardamom

½ cup rose water

Cinnamon, almonds or pistachios for garnish (optional)

1 Rinse rice in water and drain.

2 Add rice and 8 cups water to a pot and bring to a boil. Simmer covered for 20-25 minutes until rice has absorbed much of the water and is kind of soupy.

3 Add sugar, butter, saffron, cardamom, and rose water. Stir well and simmer covered for an additional 30-40 minutes, stirring occasionally to release saffron and keep mixture consistent. Add 1 cup water if needed to keep consistency pourable.

4 Once mixture has thickened to a pourable creamy pudding consistency, pour into a large bowl or individual serving bowls/ramekins.

5 Cool to room temperature, and then chill in fridge for an hour. Pudding will thicken and harden. Decorate the top with patterns of cinnamon, almonds or pistachios, if desired, before serving.

Prep time: *5 minutes,* Hands-off cooking time: *about 1 hour (with an occasional stir),* Serves 8

Per serving: 198 calories, 3 g fat, 2 g saturated fat, 2 g protein, 43 g carbs, 0 g fiber, 25 g sugar, 1 mg sodium

G Gluten Free **V** Vegetarian

Fruit Fizz

Soda is a big culprit in bad eating habits. It consists largely of chemicals, high fructose corn syrup, and caffeine. For a soda substitute, try our Fruit Fizz recipes, which use agave nectar (fruit fructose) as the sweetener. Agave nectar won't cause the same sugar spike as the typical sweeteners in commercial soda, and it dissolves readily in cold drinks, unlike honey.

Citrus Fruit Fizz

1 Tbsp lemon juice (½ lemon)

1 Tbsp lime juice (½ lime)

1 Tbsp agave nectar

1 cup sparkling mineral water

Raspberries (optional)

1 Stir juices and agave nectar together in a glass.

2 Add water.

3 For fun, add fresh raspberries as an edible garnish.

Prep time: *5 minutes,* Serves *1*
Per serving: 75 calories, 0 g fat, 0 g saturated fat,
0 g protein, 21 g carbs, 0 g fiber, 17 g sugar, 0 mg sodium

Pomegranate Fruit Fizz

⅓ cup 100% Pomegranate Juice

⅔ cup sparkling mineral water

Pomegranate seeds (optional)

1 Stir juice and mineral water in a glass.

2 Add pomegranate seeds as an edible garnish. They'll float to the top and add a festive flair.

Prep time: *5 minutes,* Serves *1*

Per serving: 47 calories, 0 g fat, 0 g saturated fat,
0 g protein, 12 g carbs, 0 g fiber, 11 g sugar,
10 mg sodium

Vanilla Chai Bread Pudding

If you recoil in fear when you see the words "ramekin" or "water bath" in a recipe, you're not alone. Many people assume those recipes are for veteran chefs, but in reality they are quite simple. Here is an easy bread pudding, flavored with Trader Joe's delicious chai mix and sweetened with a little agave nectar. If you like the flavors of chai and vanilla, you'll like this dessert.

6 cups cubed challah bread (a little more than ½ of a 1-lb challah loaf)

3 eggs

1 cup heavy cream

1 ½ Tbsp Spicy Chai Latte Mix powder

1 tsp vanilla extract

¼ cup agave nectar

Candied ginger (optional, for garnish)

Six 6-oz ramekins (3.5-inch diameter)

1 Preheat oven to 350° F.

2 Place cubed bread in medium sized bowl.

3 In a separate bowl, combine eggs, cream, chai powder, vanilla, and agave. Whisk together until mixture is smooth and all chai powder has dissolved.

4 Pour chai mixture over bread and let soak for 10 minutes. Do not stir since that will create a mush. Once or twice, using a large spoon or spatula, gently flip some of the bread over so mixture soaks in evenly.

5 Fill each well-buttered or oiled ramekin with bread mixture. Press gently to compact slightly.

6 Place ramekins in baking dish. Create a water bath by filling baking dish with hot water. Water should reach halfway up sides of ramekins.

Cooking with Trader Joe's Cookbook Companion

7 Place in oven (carefully!), drape with foil, and bake for about 30 minutes until bread pudding is firm in the center.

8 Pop out of ramekins if desired. Serve warm with ice cream, frozen yogurt, or drizzle with chocolate sauce. Garnish with pieces of candied ginger.

Prep time: *15 minutes*
Hands-off cooking time: *30 minutes,* **Serves** *6*

*Per serving: 347 calories, 19 g fat, 10 g saturated fat,
6 g protein, 36 g carbs, 1 g fiber, 16 g sugar, 227 mg sodium*

All Mixed Up Margaritas

Trader Joe's has a great Margarita Mix, but perhaps you're feeling a little more adventurous. Instead of a mix, try some of the juices we suggest below…pomegranate, pink lemonade, or sparkling lime soda to name a few. There's no substitute for fresh lime in an authentic-tasting margarita, so have plenty on hand; most importantly make sure to pick up a real lime squeezer so your friends will believe you when you claim to be a Margarita master.

¼ cup juice, such as Pink Lemonade, Pomegranate Limeade, French Market Limeade, or Just Pomegranate

½ oz (1 Tbsp) triple sec or other orange-flavored liqueur

2 oz (4 Tbsp) tequila

2 Tbsp lime juice (juice of 1 lime)

Ice cubes or crushed ice

1   If you want to salt the rim, rub rim with a cut lime and dip in a shallow dish of kosher or flaked salt. It's also fun using different kinds of sugar to coat the rim. Try Turbinado sugar with the pomegranate version, or white sugar with the Pink Lemonade version.

2   Add ingredients to a glass cup. Add enough ice to fill remainder of cup and stir.

Prep Time: *5 minutes,* Serves *1*

Per serving: 218 calories, 0 g fat, 0 g saturated fat, 0 g protein, 16 g carbs, 0 g fiber, 13 g sugar, 0 mg sodium

For a small pitcher:

1 cup juice (or 1 ½ cups if you don't want it too strong)

¼ cup triple sec

1 cup tequila

½ cup lime juice (juice of 4 limes)

3 cups ice

One Bowl Peach & Blueberry Cobbler

This may be the easiest cobbler you can make. Simply throw all the ingredients in an oven-safe dish and top with any fruit you have on hand. The result: warm fruit comfortably nestled in soft pillows of dough. Serve with whipped cream or a scoop of vanilla ice cream.

1 cup Buttermilk Pancake Mix or Bisquick

¼ cup butter, melted

½ cup sugar

⅔ cup milk

3 cups sliced peaches, drained (fresh, frozen, or canned, such as jarred Peaches in Light Syrup)

½ cup blueberries, fresh or frozen (thawed and drained if frozen)

¼ tsp ground cinnamon (optional)

1 Preheat oven to 375° F.

2 Select an 8x8-inch square ovenproof dish or a glass 9-inch pie plate for the cobbler. (If you're feeding a crowd, double the recipe and use a 9x13-inch baking dish.) Melt butter right in the baking dish and use it as a mixing bowl.

3 Add pancake mix, sugar, and milk to melted butter. Stir with a fork until just combined. Batter will be lumpy – do not over mix.

4 Scatter peaches and blueberries evenly over batter. Lightly sprinkle cinnamon evenly on top.

5 Bake for 30 minutes or until light golden brown.

Variations: Use apples, pears, or plums. Frozen and canned fruit work just as well as fresh fruit in this recipe.

Prep time: *5 minutes,*
Hands-off cooking time: *30 minutes,* Serves 4

Per serving: 389 calories, 14 g fat, 8 g saturated fat, 6 g protein, 63 g carbs, 3 g fiber, 42 g sugar, 469 mg sodium

Tarte Tatin

Tarte Tatin is the quintessential French dessert. It's an upside-down apple tart where the apples are caramelized and baked with a pastry crust on top. Once baked, the tart is flipped upside-down, revealing the fanned layer of apples on top. Most recipes for Tarte Tatin involve first melting sugar into a direct caramel in the pan. We don't like this method – it's tricky and dangerous because of the extremely hot and sticky caramel which may splatter when you try to add the apple slices. Instead, we first place the apple slices on top of the butter and sugar, cooking it until the mixture underneath caramelizes. Much easier and with the same result.

8 firm medium-sized apples, such as Granny Smith or Pink Lady

¼ cup butter

1 cup sugar

1 frozen pie crust, thawed, or 1 sheet frozen Puff Pastry

1 Preheat oven to 400° F.

2 Peel, quarter, and core apples. To keep apples from turning brown while you work, place them in a bowl of water with the juice of a couple of lemons.

3 Melt butter over medium heat in a 10-12-inch cast iron pan or other oven-safe pan. Sprinkle and spread sugar evenly over melted butter. Layer apple quarters tightly in pan, nesting them against each other. Cook on high heat for 10 minutes. You will see sugar-butter mixture bubble and caramelize.

4 Place crust on top of apples. Very carefully, making sure not to burn your fingers, tuck in crust all around edges. Pierce crust a few times.

5 Place pan in oven and bake for 30 minutes until crust is golden.

6 Let tart rest for 20 minutes. Run a knife along edge of pan to loosen crust. Flip tart onto a plate and serve warm with vanilla ice cream or crème fraîche (more traditional).

Prep and cooking time: *25 minutes*
Hands-off cooking time: *30 minutes,* Serves 8

*Per serving: 381 calories, 18 g fat, 11 g saturated fat,
2 g protein, 54 g carbs, 3 g fiber, 38 g sugar, 212 mg sodium*

Saffron Yogurt Pudding

This sweet and exotic pudding is flavored with saffron and topped with nuts and dried fruit. The Greek yogurt used as the base has a luxurious, thick texture similar to sour cream. If you can't find Greek yogurt, drain plain yogurt in a paper-towel-lined strainer for 5 hours or overnight.

1 (16-oz) container Greek style nonfat plain yogurt

½ tsp Spanish Saffron threads (¼ the jar), or use ground saffron and omit water

2 tsp hot water

½ cup sugar

¼ cup pistachios or almonds

Dried fruit or dried hibiscus flowers as garnish (optional)

1 In a small bowl, combine saffron and hot water. Let sit for 10 minutes for color and flavor to be released.

2 Combine yogurt, saffron mixture, and sugar and mix well.

3 Place yogurt in 4 serving bowls, and store in refrigerator until ready to serve. Top each bowl with 1 Tbsp nuts and garnish with dried fruit.

Prep time: *5 minutes*, Serves 4

G Gluten Free · V Vegetarian

Per serving: 207 calories, 3 g fat, 0 g saturated fat,
13 g protein, 32 g carbs, 1 g fiber, 29 g sugar, 41 mg sodium

Sour Cream Cheesecake

Those who can barely stomach a serving of regular cheesecake will love the fact that this one is light and not too sweet. It's perfect for a big party — just cut into squares, place into cupcake paper liners, and garnish with fresh berries. Delightful finger food!

1 ½ cups crushed graham crackers

6 Tbsp melted butter

½ tsp cinnamon

1 (8-oz) block light or regular cream cheese, softened

1 tsp vanilla

¼ cup + ⅓ cup sugar

2 eggs

1 (16-oz) container light or regular sour cream

Berries for garnish (optional)

1 Preheat oven to 350° F.

2 Mix graham cracker crumbs, butter, cinnamon and ginger. Press into a 9-inch pan or springform pan.

3 In a mixer, whip cream cheese, vanilla, and ¼ cup sugar until smooth. Add eggs and beat until mixed. Pour on top of graham cracker crust and bake for 20 minutes. Remove from oven.

4 Blend sour cream and ⅓ cup sugar. Pour on top of cream cheese layer, and bake for an additional 10 minutes.

5 Remove from heat and allow to cool. Refrigerate at least 4 hours. Garnish with berries if desired.

Prep time: *20 minutes,*
Hands-off cooking time: *30 minutes,* Serves 10

*Per serving: 297 calories, 23 g fat, 15 g saturated fat,
5 g protein, 18 g carbs, 0 g fiber, 16 g sugar, 145 mg sodium*

Honey, I Ate the Chocolate Bread Pudding

Cold vanilla ice cream melting on warm bread pudding is one of those feel-good dessert combinations. And this recipe makes a happy cook as well. Just 3 ingredients... toss it all in and bake. Trader Joe's also makes Whole Wheat Orange or White Orange versions of the bread used in this recipe, which can be substituted. Serve warm with vanilla ice cream. Or if you really want to be indulgent (we encourage it), serve with chocolate ice cream.

½ loaf (8 slices) Whole Wheat Honey Bread

1 ½ cups Brownie Truffle Baking Mix (just the dry mix, don't add anything else)

2 ½ cups whole milk

1 Cut crusts off bread slices. Cube bread into ½-inch by ½-inch pieces. Toss diced bread in an 8x8-inch lightly greased or buttered baking pan and arrange so pan is filled evenly.

2 Combine milk and brownie mix. Stir well for a minute until dissolved. Pour brownie mixture over diced bread. Lightly press down on bread pieces so that they are thoroughly soaked through with brownie liquid.

3 Set pan aside while you preheat oven to 350° F, perhaps 10 minutes or so. This extra time will give the bread time to soak further. Cover pan tightly with foil and bake for 30 minutes.

4 When done, remove pan from oven and let it cool for 15 minutes, allowing bread pudding to set. Serve warm.

Prep time: *5-10 minutes,*
Hands-off cooking time: *30 minutes,* Serves 9

Per serving: 272 calories, 5 g fat, 3 g saturated fat,
7 g protein, 56 g carbs, 4 g fiber, 29 g sugar, 201 mg sodium

Lemon Tart with Fresh Berries

Lemon curd is an English specialty spread, creamy and rich with the flavor of fresh lemons. Fresh fruit is a nice balance to the tang of lemon curd. For an easy tart, spread the lemon curd on a cooked pastry crust and top with fresh berries (and even ice cream or whipped cream). This tart will last just fine in the fridge and can be made ahead of time. Keep a jar of lemon curd in the pantry and a pie crust in the freezer, ready to go as a last minute dessert. If the Queen drops by for high tea, you'll be prepared.

1 frozen pie crust

1 (10.5-oz) jar Lemon Curd

Fresh seasonal berries

1 Thaw crust and press into an 11-inch tart pan or shallow pie pan. Bake according to single-crust instructions on box.

2 Remove crust from oven and cool completely.

3 Spread lemon curd in an even layer across baked crust. Fill with berries. Chill for later, or serve right away.

Prep and cooking time: *15 minutes (not counting cooling time),* **Serves 6**

Per serving: 409 calories, 21 g fat, 12 g saturated fat, 5 g protein, 50 g carbs, 1 g fiber, 32 g sugar, 305 mg sodium

Strawberry Frozen Yogurt

This strawberry fro-yo is made with just 3 ingredients: strawberries, yogurt, and sugar. You'll be pleasantly surprised by the explosive strawberry flavor. Trader Joe's has frozen strawberries year-round. which are a convenient option for this recipe. Trader Joe's Greek yogurt gives it extra creaminess, but you can use plain regular yogurt as well. An ice cream maker is necessary for this recipe. For vanilla fro-yo, omit strawberries and add ½ tsp vanilla.

4-5 cups fresh or frozen strawberries

2 cups Greek yogurt or plain yogurt

⅓ cup sugar

1 Freeze ice cream maker bowl overnight.

2 Place strawberries and sugar in a blender. Purée until mixture is bright red and smooth. You can pulse and make it chunky if you prefer.

3 Mix in yogurt and stir until well combined. Place in fridge for 1-2 hours until fully chilled.

4 Place mixture in ice cream maker according to manufacturer instructions.

Prep time: *10 minutes (not counting time to chill in fridge)*
Hands-off churning time: *25 minutes (varies by ice cream maker manufacturer)*, **Serves** 6

Per serving: 127 calories, 2 g fat, 1 g saturated fat, 5 g protein, 25 g carbs, 2 g fiber, 22 g sugar, 59 mg sodium

Mango Lassi

A mango lassi is basically a smoothie made with yogurt and mango. Flaxseed oil is optional if you want to add some healthy omega-3 essential fatty acids to your morning. Don't worry when you read the word "fatty" – omega-3's increase your body's metabolic rate, actually helping to burn excess fats in your body! You'll find flaxseed oil in the supplements section at Trader Joe's, not with the oils.

1 cup frozen Mango Chunks

1 cup plain or vanilla yogurt (nonfat or regular)

¼ cup orange juice

1 tsp agave nectar or honey

1 Tbsp flaxseed oil (optional)

1 Add ingredients to a blender and blend until smooth.

Prep time: *5 minutes,* Serves *2*

Per serving: 132 calories, 0 g fat, 0 g saturated fat, 6 g protein, 28 g carbs, 2 g fiber, 26 g sugar, 82 mg sodium

Coconut Cream Cake

A fellow Trader Joe's fan sent us a recipe for coconut cake, which inspired this version of the Venezuelan classic dessert, *Bien Me Sabe de Coco* ("tastes good to me"). In Venezuela, it is served cold, straight out of the fridge, and it is a wet cake. The cake mix at Trader Joe's is much more dense than the sponge cake used for *Bien Me Sabe*, so the pudding doesn't soak into the cake, but is more like a cream filling. For a more traditional version, use sponge cake.

Cake:

1 box Vanilla Cake & Baking Mix

1 cup Light Coconut Milk (half a can)

2 eggs

½ cup butter, melted

Coconut cream filling:

3 cups Light Coconut Milk (buy 2 cans total: 1 cup for cake, remaining 3 cups coconut milk for pudding filling)

⅓ cup sugar

3 Tbsp cornstarch

Pinch of salt

3 egg yolks, lightly beaten

Frosting:

1 cup heavy whipping cream

2 Tbsp sugar

Coconut flakes (optional)

1 Bake cake according to package instructions, using coconut milk instead of milk. Let cake cool for at least 10 minutes (a hot cake will break more easily), and then remove cake from pan. This cake tends to stick, so loosen carefully. Let cake cool completely, and then slice in half horizontally.

2 To make coconut pudding, place sugar, cornstarch, and salt in a saucepan. Add a few spoonfuls of coconut milk and stir until well mixed. This allows cornstarch to dissolve, thus avoiding lumps. Add remaining coconut milk. Place over medium heat, stirring frequently, until mixture thickens. Cook for 2 minutes, stirring constantly. Remove from heat.

3 Take a few spoonfuls of hot pudding and stir into egg yolks. This tempers the yolks and slowly warms them up, so that they don't cook too quickly. Pour egg mixture into hot pudding mixture and return to heat, stirring constantly. Cook just a minute longer. Allow pudding to cool slightly.

4 To assemble cake, place cake bottom back into the pan you used to bake the cake. Pour pudding on top and spread evenly. Place the other half on top. Store in fridge for at least 4 hours or overnight.

5 Whip heavy cream and sugar until soft peaks form. Frost cake, and sprinkle liberally with coconut flakes.

Prep and cooking time: *25 minutes*
Hands-off cooking time: *40 minutes,* Serves *9*

Per serving: 510 calories, 30 g fat, 18 g saturated fat,
4 g protein, 59 g carbs, 2 g fiber, 35 g sugar, 447 mg sodium

Chocolate Coffee Fudge

Mango Passion Fruit Cocktail

A touch of exotic sweetness takes us to faraway beaches with just one sip. Enjoy these cocktails while watching the sunset on a warm day.

For each drink:

⅓ cup Mango Passion Fruit Blend or Mango Nectar, chilled

⅔ cup champagne or sparkling mineral water, chilled

Fresh raspberries or currants

1 Add a few fresh raspberries or currants to each glass.

2 Pour in fruit juice and champagne. Stir to combine.

Tip: For champagnes, try Gloria Ferrer Sonoma Brut, Piper Sonoma Brut, or splurge for the sublime Veuve Clicquot Ponsardin Brut.

Prep time: 5 minutes, **Serves** 1

Per serving: 109 calories, 0 g fat, 0 g saturated fat,
0 g protein, 13 g carbs, 0 g fiber, 10 g sugar, 8 mg sodium

Gluten Free   Vegetarian

Chocolate Coffee Fudge

This rich fudge is ridiculously easy – only 3 ingredients and a few minutes to prepare. Wona sent this fudge to her husband's office for a chocolate-themed contest, and it won, beating out a multitude of extravagant desserts. When she was asked for the recipe, she was almost embarrassed to share it given how simple it is! A hint of coffee enhances the taste of chocolate and lifts it to new flavor highs. Try adding a small amount of instant coffee the next time you make a chocolate dessert.

1 (14-oz) can sweetened condensed milk

2 Tbsp instant coffee

½ Tbsp water

1 (12-oz) bag semi-sweet chocolate chips

1 Heat condensed milk in a heavy saucepan over medium heat.

2 Dissolve instant coffee in water (it will be thick) and stir into condensed milk.

3 Add chocolate chips, reduce flame to low, and stir until melted and smooth. Be careful not to scorch fudge.

4 Pour into an oiled 8x8-inch pan. Chill in fridge until set, about 2 hours.

Tip: When cutting fudge, a plastic knife is easiest. If using a regular knife, wipe it clean in between cuts. Then use a spatula to lift out pieces. You can also line pan with wax paper for easier removal.

Prep time: *5-10 minutes,* **Makes about** *20 small pieces*

Per piece: 154 calories, 6 g fat, 4 g saturated fat, 3 g protein, 23 g carbs, 1 g fiber, 20 g sugar, 20 mg sodium

Breakfast Beginnings

Baked French Toast Casserole

For those weekend mornings when you have time for a more leisurely breakfast, try this twist on traditional French toast. This dish is easy enough for a casual family breakfast and elegant enough for an upscale brunch. It's quick to assemble, and you don't have to stand over the stove cooking each piece individually.

....

1 (1-lb) challah loaf or brioche loaf

2 cups whole milk

4 eggs

1 tsp cinnamon

2 tsp vanilla extract

¼ cup brown sugar

1 Tbsp Turbinado sugar for sprinkling on top

....

1 Preheat oven to 350° F.

2 Oil or butter a 9x13-inch glass baking dish (use an 8x8-inch dish if using a smaller loaf).

3 Tear loaf into bite-size pieces and place in pan.

4 Whisk together milk, eggs, cinnamon, vanilla, and brown sugar. Pour mixture over bread.

5 Wait a few minutes to let the liquid soak into the bread, gently tossing bread around a little to soak evenly. Sprinkle top with sugar.

6 Bake in oven for 35-40 minutes, uncovered. It will puff up when done.

Prep time: *10 minutes,*
Hands-off cooking time: *35-40 minutes,* **Serves 8**

Per serving: 279 calories, 9 g fat, 2 g saturated fat, 9 g protein, 41 g carbs, 2 g fiber, 13 g sugar, 321 mg sodium

Hangover Hash

This dish is reminiscent of those greasy spoon diners that are popular for post-party grub. Hash brown patties, ready to go, are combined with Canadian bacon, bell peppers, and onion for a hearty breakfast. To put the finishing touch on this dish, top with a sunny side up egg. And, don't forget the coffee.

5 frozen hash brown patties, thawed and cut into ½-inch cubes

1 Tbsp olive oil

½ cup diced onion

1 (6-oz) pkg Canadian bacon, cubed (about 1 ¼ cups) or cubed ham

1 cup diced bell peppers

1 Heat olive oil over medium-high heat. Using a cast-iron skillet will ensure a nice crispness to the hash, but a regular skillet is fine too.

2 Cook onions until translucent, about 3 minutes.

3 Add remaining ingredients and cook for another 5 minutes, stirring occasionally. Hash browns will crumble as you cook. Let some of them brown for a nice crispness throughout the hash.

4 Serve immediately with ketchup and/or hot sauce (optional).

Prep and cooking time: *10 minutes, Serves 2*

Per serving: 521 calories, 26 g fat, 2 g saturated fat, 15 g protein, 55 g carbs, 9 g fiber, 5 g sugar, 1291 mg sodium

Homemade Granola

A homemade granola recipe might not sound like something you would find in a book written for Trader Joe's fans. After all, Trader Joe's sells granola, ready-to-go. But making granola is easy, economical, and a practical way to use up leftover nuts and dried fruit. Adding the dried fruit at the end keeps it from getting burned while the granola bakes in the oven. Enjoy the granola with yogurt, as a cereal with milk, or just by itself - it makes a great snack at home, at the office, or to take camping.

4 cups regular rolled oats

1 ½ cups nuts, such as almonds, walnuts, or pine nuts

½ cup sunflower seeds or pepitas

¼ cup flax seeds (optional)

1 tsp cinnamon

¾ cup honey

¼ cup neutral/plain oil, such as grapeseed oil

1 tsp vanilla

½ tsp salt

1 cup dried fruits, such as apricots, berries, mango, dates, or raisins

1 Preheat oven to 300° F.

2 In a large bowl, combine oats, nuts, seeds, and cinnamon.

3 In a small saucepan over medium low heat, stir honey, oil, vanilla, and salt until honey has dissolved.

4 Pour honey mixture over oat mixture and stir well until evenly combined and coated.

5 Lightly spray or coat a baking pan or baking sheet with oil. Spread granola mixture on the pan.

6 Place in oven and bake for about 20-25 minutes, gently moving/stirring the granola every 10 minutes so that it bakes evenly. Keep an eye on it to make sure it isn't getting overly toasted. When oats are light brown, it's done.

7 Granola will still look/be sticky when you take it out of the oven, but it will dry and harden as it cools.

8 When cooled, add dried fruit. Store in a container. It will keep for 1 week (4 weeks in fridge).

Prep time: *10 minutes*
Hands-off cooking time: *25 minutes*
Makes *7 cups of granola*

Per ½-cup serving: 330 calories, 17 g fat,
1 g saturated fat, 7 g protein, 42 g carbs, 4 g fiber,
19 g sugar, 85 mg sodium

* Use GF oats

Hey Huevos Rancheros

Amigo, do you like a breakfast with more of a kick? Spice things up with this satisfying Mexican-style egg dish. On the side, serve black beans topped with a dollop of yogurt, slices of avocado and tomato, or fresh fruit.

2 eggs

2 small corn tortillas

Salt to taste

1 Tbsp guacamole, such as Avocado's Number Guacamole

1 Tbsp salsa, such as Chunky Salsa

1 Tbsp yogurt or sour cream

1 Warm tortillas in a pan and set aside.

2 Heat a lightly oiled nonstick skillet over medium-high heat. Gently crack eggs into pan, taking care to keep yolks whole. Sprinkle with a pinch of salt. Decrease heat to low and cover pan. Cook eggs only until whites are set and yolk has thickened but is not yet hard.

3 Place one egg inside each tortilla, topping with guacamole, salsa, and yogurt.

Prep time and cooking time: *5-10 minutes*
Serves *1*

Per serving: 352 calories, 15 g fat, 4 g saturated fat, 18 g protein, 34 g carbs, 5 g fiber, 5 g sugar, 410 mg sodium

Egg Muffin Breakfast Sandwich

In the time it takes to hit the drive-through for a breakfast sandwich, you can make a healthier version yourself. It's easy to make dozens of variations on this basic sandwich. Switch it up with ready-made guacamole, salsa, and Mexican cheese. For a vegetarian version, replace the meat with a veggie burger or soy sausage patty (both available in the frozen aisle at Trader Joe's). Add baby spinach or avocado slices. Slice up fragrant ripe tomatoes on a plain egg sandwich and sprinkle with salt.

1 large egg

1 whole wheat English muffin

1 slice sharp cheddar cheese

1 slice Canadian style bacon, or soy sausage patty

Salt and pepper to taste

1 Lightly spray or oil a skillet over medium-high heat. Toast muffin face down until heated through. Set open halves aside and place cheese on one half. It will start to melt from the heat.

2 Over high heat, break egg and slowly release it onto the pan so that it doesn't spread too quickly. Allow the white to set up a bit (a minute or less), sprinkling on a bit of salt and pepper if desired. Lower heat to medium, toss in a tablespoon of water, and cover pan tightly. Allow egg to cook 30 seconds or more, monitoring carefully to get the yolk how you like it. Don't overcook! Stack egg on top of cheese.

3 Heat Canadian bacon and add to the stack, topping off with the other muffin half.

Prep and cooking time: *5-10 minutes*
Makes *one sandwich*

Per sandwich: 324 calories, 16 g fat,
7 g saturated fat, 22 g protein, 27 g carbs,
5 g fiber, 2 g sugar, 597 mg sodium

* Use veggie burger
or soy sauage patty

Quick and Creamy Quinoa Cereal

Quinoa (pronounced KEEN-wah) is a nice alternative to oatmeal. High in protein and gluten free, quinoa is super healthy and has a nice "seedy" texture and a nutty taste. Start with our recipe below and then experiment with your own additions.

1 cup uncooked quinoa, rinsed and drained

2 cups water

1 ripe banana, peeled and diced

½ tsp cinnamon

½ tsp vanilla extract or flavoring

½ cup dried berries, such as Golden Berry Blend or Dried Berry Medley

¼ cup slivered almonds

1 Add quinoa, water, banana, cinnamon, and vanilla to a small saucepan. Bring to a simmer and cook for 15 minutes or until all the water is absorbed.

2 Mix in nuts and dried berries. Top with cream, milk, honey, Turbinado sugar, or maple syrup as desired.

Prep time: *5 minutes*
Hands-off cooking time: *15 minutes, Serves 4*

Per serving: 315 calories, 7 g fat, 0 g saturated fat, 8 g protein, 58 g carbs, 6 g fiber, 21 g sugar, 5 mg sodium

Mushroom Basil Frittata

A frittata is similar to a quiche, but without the crust. You can use virtually any ingredients you have on hand—a great way to use up leftover veggies. This version uses criminis, which are actually baby Portobello mushrooms. They are richer in flavor and nutrients than regular white button mushrooms. For a milder flavor, you can use white button mushrooms or another variety of your choice. This versatile dish can be served around the clock. It's great for breakfast with a warm mug of coffee, or for dinner with a green salad.

3 cups fresh Sliced Crimini Mushrooms

3 Tbsp butter

8 eggs

⅓ cup whole milk or heavy cream

½ tsp salt

¼ tsp black pepper

½ cup fresh basil leaves, roughly chopped

½ cup Quattro Formaggio shredded cheese

1 Preheat oven to 350°F.

2 Melt butter in a 10-inch nonstick oven-safe skillet over medium heat. Add mushrooms and cook for 5 minutes.

3 While mushrooms are cooking, whisk eggs, milk, salt, and pepper until combined. Mix in basil and cheese.

4 Pour egg mixture into hot skillet, over the cooked mushrooms. Place in oven for 30 minutes or until egg is set. Eggs will puff up while cooking but will deflate when you take the frittata out of the oven.

Prep time: *10 minutes*
Hands-off cooking time: *30 minutes*, Serves *6*

Per serving: 235 calories, 20 g fat, 10 g saturated fat, 12 g protein, 3 g carbs, 0 g fiber, 1 g sugar, 368 mg sodium

Super-Food Fruit Smoothie

We love a good smoothie as a healthful and easy way to start the day. This particular smoothie is primarily fruit and yogurt based, but has a few nice additions that round it out. The protein in tofu and yogurt balance out the fruit carbohydrates, and the various textures work to give a nice smooth end result. Flax oil is a viable source of essential fatty acids, and Very Green powder packs a punch of vegetable minerals, vitamins, enzymes, and antioxidants.

1 ripe banana, peeled

1 cup plain yogurt

½ cup frozen blueberries

1 cup frozen Mango Chunks

⅓ cup Organic Tofu or other soft/regular tofu (about a ¾-inch slice off the end)

1 Tbsp Very Green powdered supplement

2 Tbsp flax oil

1 Tbsp honey

½ cup rice milk or your choice of milk.

1 Add all ingredients to a blender. Blend for a couple of minutes or until smooth.

2 For a delicious smoothie bowl with a little added crunch, pour in a bowl and top with a few Tbsp of granola, such as Granola & the 3 Berries, and some fresh berries.

Tip: If you have a popsicle mold, a great way to use leftover smoothies is to make smoothie pops. It's a big hit on summer days!

Prep time: *10 minutes,* **Serves** *4 (6-oz cups)*

Per serving: 219 calories, 9 g fat, 1 g saturated fat, 8 g protein, 29 g carbs, 2 g fiber, 21 g sugar, 59 mg sodium

Avocado Smoothie

This smoothie is a twist on avocado smoothies that are popular in Southeast Asia, using sweetened condensed milk as the sweetener. Avocados, once shunned because they were thought to be full of fat, are now back on the good list. That's because most of the fat in avocados is monosaturated — the "good fat" that helps to lower cholesterol. A single avocado delivers 11 grams of fiber! So don't be afraid to indulge regularly in this wonderful fruit.

1 large ripe avocado

2 cups skim milk

2 tsp honey or agave nectar

1 Scoop out flesh of avocado into a blender. Add ½ cup milk and honey. Blend until mixture is creamy and smooth.

2 Add remaining milk and mix until blended.

Variation: For a dairy-free version, use rice milk, soy milk, or almond milk, available in many varieties at Trader Joe's.

Prep time: *5 minutes,* **Serves 2**

Per serving: 272 calories, 16 g fat, 2 g saturated fat, 11 g protein, 26 g carbs, 7 g fiber, 18 g sugar, 107 mg sodium

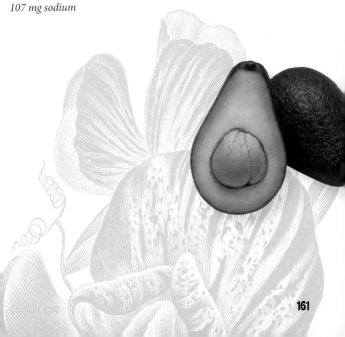

Cooking with Trader Joe's Cookbook Companion

Index

A

Ahi Tuna on Lemon Pappardelle, Seared, 70
All Mixed Up Margaritas, 136
Alla Checca, Pasta, 93
Almond-crusted Pork Tenderloin, 51
Alphabet Soup with Meatballs, Souper Fast, 35
Anytime Mediterranean Pasta, 40
Apple Tart Tartin, 138
Apricot Baked Brie, 15
Artichoke Wrap, Turkey, 81
Arugula
    Salad, Sweet Corn and, 34
    Salad with Pine Nuts and Parmesan, 20
Asian Dumpling Soup, 24
Asian Slaw, Spicy, 23
Avocado Smoothie, 161

B

Bake/Baked
    Brie, Apricot, 15
    Eggplant Zucchini, 105
    French Toast Casserole, 152
    Sweet Potato Fries, 118
Barbecue Chicken Pasta, 60
Basic Lemonade, 130
Basil Cake, Lemon, 129
Bean Soup, Black, 21
Bean Salad, Roasted Corn and, 33
Beef Stew, 96
Beet and Endive Salad, 25
Berries, Lemon Tart with Fresh, 143
Black Bean
    Cornbread, 100
    Soup, 21
BLT Sandwich, Turkey, 75
Blueberry Cobbler, One-Bowl Peach and, 137
Bread
    Garlic, 114
    Olive-stuffed, 108
    Pudding, Vanilla Chai, 134
    Pudding, Honey, I Ate the Chocolate, 142
Breakfast Sandwich, Egg Muffin, 157
Brie, Apricot Baked, 15

Bowl, Couscous, 38
Broccoli
    Slaw, Crunchy, 108
    Soup, Cream of, 29
    Squares, 102
Broiled Salmon, Soyaki, 72
Bruschetta Crackers, Goat Cheese, 18
Brussels Sprouts, Pan-Toasted, 113
Burrito, Southwest, 46
Butternut Squash Soup, Cozy, 28

Cake
    Coconut Cream, 146
    Lemon Basil, 129
Cardamom Lemonade, Honey, 131
Casserole, Enchilada, 64
Chai Bread Pudding, Vanilla, 134
Cheese Bruschetta Crackers, Goat, 18
Cheesecake, Sour Cream, 141
Chicken
    Chutney-stuffed, 50
    Go Go Mango, 43
    Honey Mustard, 82
    Just Chicken, Your Own, 98
    Lime Grilled, 61
    Pasta, Barbecue, 60
    Stew, Greek, 48
    Tandoori, 47
    Tortilla Soup, 32
Chili, Chipotle Turkey, 71
Chipotle Turkey Chili, 71
Chocolate
    Coffee Fudge, 149
    Custard, Decadent, 122
    Bread Pudding, Honey I Ate the, 142
    No Moo Mousse, 126
Chutney-stuffed Chicken, 50
Cilantro Jasmine Rice, 106
Citrus Fruit Fizz, 133
Classic Lasagna, 58
Cobbler, One-Bowl Peach & Blueberry, 137
Cock-a-leekie Soup, 27
Cocktail, Mango Passion Fruit, 148

Coconut
    Cream Cake, 146
    Curried Vegetables, 101
    Rice with Mango, 125
Coffee Fudge, Chocolate, 149
Corn
    and Arugula Salad, Sweet, 34
    and Bean Salad, Roasted, 33
    Sauteed Sweet Corn with Pine Nuts, 119
Cornbread, Black Bean, 100
Couscous Bowl, 38
Cozy Butternut Squash Soup, 28
Crackers, Goat Cheese Bruschetta, 18
Cream of Broccoli Soup, 29
Creamy Lemony Linguine, 92
Creole, Shrimp, 54
Crunchy Broccoli Slaw, 108
Crusted Fish, Herb, 41
Cucumber Yogurt Dip (Raita), 115
Curried Vegetables, Coconut, 101
Curry, Veggie Thai Yellow, 53
Custard, Decadent Chocolate, 122

D

Decadent Chocolate Custard, 122
Dumpling Soup, Asian, 24

E

Easy Shepherd's Pie, 68
Egg(s)
    Hey Huevos Rancheros, 156
    Muffin Breakfast Sandwich, 157
    Mushroom Basil Frittata, 159
    Salad Olovieh (Persian Egg Salad), 84
Eggplant
    Parmesan, 56
    Zucchini Bake, 105
Enchilada Casserole, 64
Endive Salad, Beet and, 25

F

Fiery Mango Mahi-Mahi, 52

Fish

    Fiery Mango Mahi-Mahi, 52

    Herb Crusted Fish, 41

    Lemon Sole, 57

    Seared Ahi Tuna on Lemon Pappardelle, 70

    Salmon in Puff Pastry, 94

    Soyaki Broiled Salmon, 72

Flatbread, Herbed Mushroom and Onion, 104

French Toast Casserole, Baked, 152

Fries, Baked Sweet Potato, 118

Frittata, Mushroom Basil, 159

Frozen Yogurt, Strawberry, 144

Fruit

    Fizz, Citrus, 133

    Salad, Honey Mint, 123

Fudge, Chocolate Coffee, 149

G

Garlic

    Bread, 114

    Roasted, 16

Gnocchi

    with Pancetta & Peas, Okey-, 80

    with Spinach, Gnutmeg, 90

Gnutmeg Gnocchi with Spinach, 90

Go Go Mango Chicken, 43

Goat Cheese Bruschetta Crackers, 18

Gorgonzola Herb Salad, Strawberry and, 22

Grains Vegetable Soup, Harvest, 30

Granola, Homemade, 154

Greek Chicken Stew, 48

Grilled Chicken, Lime, 61

Gyoza Salad, 73

H

Hangover Hash, 153

Harvest Grains Vegetable Soup, 30

Hash, Hangover, 153

Herb
  Crusted Fish, 41
  Mushroom and Onion Flatbread, 104
  Salad, Strawberry and Gorgonzola, 22
Hey Huevos Rancheros, 156
Homemade
  Granola, 154
  Hummos, 10
Honey
  Cardamom Lemonade, 131
  I Ate the Chocolate Bread Pudding, 142
  Mint Fruit Salad, 123
  Mustard Chicken, 82
Huevos Rancheros, Hey, 156
Hummos, Homemade, 10
Hurry for Curry: Veggie Thai Yellow Curry, 53

I

Indian Spinach Pizza, 14
Italian Wedding Soup, 36

J

Just Chicken, Your Own, 98
Just like your Mawmaw's Shrimp Creole, 54
Just Peachy Pie, 128

K

Kabobs, Turkish Minted, 66

L

Lasagna
  Classic, 58
  Saag Paneer, 74
Lassi, Mango, 145
Lemon
  Basil Cake, 129
  Citrus Fruit Fizz, 133
  Linguine, Creamy, 92
  Pappardelle, Seared Ahi Tuna on, 70
  Sole, 57
  Tart with Fresh Berries, 143
Lemonade
  Basic, 130
  Honey Cardamom, 131

Lentil Salad, Mediterranean, 26
Lime Grilled Chicken, 61

M

Mahi-Mahi, Fiery Mango, 52
Mango
    Chicken, Go Go, 43
    Coconut Rice with, 125
    Lassi, 145
    Mahi-Mahi, Fiery, 52
    Passion Fruit Cocktail, 148
    Salad, Shrimp, 87
Margaritas, All Mixed Up, 136
Meatballs, Souper Fast Alphabet Soup with, 35
Meatloaves, Mini-, 76
Mediterranean
    Lentil Salad, 26
    Pasta, Anytime, 40
Mini-Meatloaves, 76
Minted Kabobs, Turkish, 66
Moussaka, Vegetarian Mushroom, 62
Mousse, No Moo, 126
Mozarella Skewers, Tomato and, 11
Mushroom
    Basil Frittata, 159
    Moussaka, Vegetarian, 62
    and Onion Flatbread, Herbed, 104
Mustard Chicken, Honey, 82

N

No Moo Mousse, 126
Noodles, Peanutty Sesame, 91
Nutty Wild Rice Salad, 86

O

Okey-Gnocchi with Pancetta & Peas, 80
Olive-stuffed Bread, 108
Olovieh (Persian), Egg Salad, 84
One-Bowl Peach & Blueberry Cobbler, 137

P

Pan-Toasted Brussels Sprouts, 113

Pancetta & Peas, Okey-Gnocchi with, 80

Parmesan, Eggplant, 56

Passion Fruit Cocktail, Mango, 148

Pasta

    Alla Checca, 93

    Anytime Mediterranean, 40

    Barbecue Chicken, 60

    Creamy Lemony Linguine, 92

    Couscous Bowl, 38

    Saag Paneer Lasagna, 74

    Salad, Spinach Pesto, 65

    with Sun Dried Tomatoes, Stir-Fried, 79

Peach/Peachy

    and Blueberry Cobbler, One-Bowl, 137

    Quesadilla, 67

    Sangria, 124

    Pie, Just, 128

Peanutty Sesame Noodles, 91

Pesto Pasta Salad, Spinach, 65

Pie

    Easy Shepherd's, 68

    Just Peachy, 128

    Tarte Tatin, 138

Pine Nuts

    and Parmesan, Arugula Salad with, 20

    Sauteed Sweet Corn with, 119

Pizza

    Bianca with Prosciutto and Asparagus, 83

    Indian Spinach, 14

    Rosemary Potato, 107

Pork Tenderloin, Almond-crusted, 51

Portobellos, Spinach & Feta Stuffed Baby, 110

Potato Pizza, Rosemary, 107

Prosciutto

    and Asparagus, Pizza Bianca with, 83

    Scallops wrapped with, 17

Pudding

    Honey, I Ate the Chocolate Bread, 142

    Saffron Rice, 132

    Saffron Yogurt, 140

    Vanilla Chai Bread, 134

Puff Pastry, Salmon in, 94

Q

Quesadillas
    Peachy, 67
    Smoked Salmon, 12
Quiche
    Simply, 42
    Mini-quiche, Spinach Timbales, 116
Quinoa Cereal, Quick and Creamy, 158

R

Raita Cucumber Yogurt Dip, 115
Rice
    Cilantro Jasmine, 106
    Pudding, Saffron, 132
    with Mango, Coconut, 125
Roasted Corn and Bean Salad, 33
Roasted Garlic, 16
Rosemary Potato Pizza, 107

S

Saag Paneer Lasagna, 74
Saffron
    Rice Pudding, 132
    Yogurt Pudding, 140
Salad
    Beet and Endive, 25
    Crunchy Broccoli Slaw, 108
    Egg Salad Olovieh (Persian), 84
    Gyoza, 73
    Mediterranean Lentil, 26
    Nutty Wild Rice, 86
    Roasted Corn and Bean, 33
    Shrimp Mango, 87
    Spinach Pesto Pasta, 65
    Strawberry and Gorgonzola Herb, 22
    Sweet Corn and Arugula, 34
    with Pine Nuts and Parmesan, Arugula, 20
Salmon
    in Puff Pastry, 94
    Quesadillas, Smoked, 12
    Soyaki Broiled, 72

Sandwich,
    Egg Muffin Breakfast, 157
    Turkey BLT, 75
Sangria, Peachy, 124
Sauteed Sweet Corn with Pine Nuts, 119
Scallops, Prosciutto-wrapped, 17
Scampi, Shrimp, 95
Seared Ahi Tuna on Lemon Pappardelle, 70
Sesame Noodles, Peanutty, 91
Shepherd's Pie, Easy, 68
Shrimp
    Boats, Spicy Tropical, 13
    Creole, Just like your Mawmaw's, 54
    Mango Salad, 87
    Scampi, 95
    Soup, Spicy, 31
Simply Quiche, 42
Skewers, Tomato and Mozzarella, 11
Slaw
    Crunchy Broccoli, 108
    Spicy Asian, 23
Smoked Salmon Quesadillas, 12
Smoothie
    Avocado, 161
    Super-Food Fruit, 160
Sole, Lemon, 57
Soyaki Broiled Salmon, 72
Soup
    Asian Dumpling, 24
    Black Bean, 21
    Chicken Tortilla, 32
    Cock-a-leekie, 27
    Cozy Butternut Squash, 28
    Cream of Broccoli, 29
    Harvest Grains Vegetable, 30
    Italian Wedding, 36
    Spicy Shrimp, 31
    with Meatballs, Souper Fast Alphabet Soup, 35
Souper Fast Alphabet Soup with Meatballs, 35
Sour Cream Cheesecake, 141
Southwest Burrito, 46
Spicy Asian Slaw, 23
Spicy Shrimp Soup, 31
Spicy Tropical Shrimp Boats, 13

Spinach
    and Feta Stuffed Baby Portobellos, 110
    Pesto Pasta Salad, 65
    Pizza, Indian, 14
    Timbales (crustless Mini-Quiche), 116
    with Attitude, Wilted, 112
Squares, Broccoli, 102
Squash
    Soup, Cozy Butternut, 28
    Strata, Summer, 88
Stew
    Beef, 96
    Greek Chicken, 48
Stir-Fried Pasta with Sun Dried Tomatoes, 79
Stir Fry, Sweet and Sour Tofu, 44
Strata, Summer Squash, 88
Strawberry
    and Gorgonzola Herb Salad, 22
    Frozen Yogurt, 144
Stuffed
    Baby Portobellos, Spinach & Feta, 110
    Bread, Olive-, 108
    Chicken, Chutney-, 50
Summer Squash Strata, 88
Sun Dried Tomatoes, Stir-Fried Pasta with, 79
Super-Food Fruit Smoothie, 160
Sweet and Sour Tofu Stir Fry, 44
Sweet Corn and Arugula Salad, 34
Sweet Potato Fries, Baked, 118

T

Tandoori Chicken, 47
Tart with Fresh Berries, Lemon, 143
Tarte Tatin, 138
Tenderloin, Almond-crusted Pork, 51
Thai Yellow Curry, Veggie, 53
Tikka Masala, Vegetable, 78
Timbales, Spinach (crustless mini-quiche), 116
Tofu Stir Fry, Sweet and Sour, 44
Tomato and Mozzarella Skewers, 10
Tortilla Soup, Chicken, 32
Tropical Shrimp Boats, Spicy, 13
Tuna on Lemon Pappardelle, Seared Ahi, 70

Turkey
> Artichoke Wrap, 81
> BLT Sandwich, 75
> Chili, Chipotle, 71
Turkish Minted Kabobs, 66

V

Vanilla Chai Bread Pudding, 134
Vegetable
> Soup, Harvest Grains, 30
> Tikka Masala, 78
Vegetables, Coconut Curried, 101
Vegetarian Mushroom Moussaka, 62
Veggie Thai Yellow Curry, 53

W

Wedding Soup, Italian, 36
Wild Rice Salad, Nutty, 86
Wilted Spinach with Attitude, 112
Wrap, Turkey Artichoke, 81

Y

Yellow Curry, Veggie Thai, 53
Yogurt
> Dip, Cucumber (Raita), 115
> Pudding, Saffron, 140
> Strawberry Frozen, 144
Your Own Just Chicken, 98

Z

Zucchini Bake, Eggplant, 105

Trader Joe's
Store Locations

ARIZONA

Ahwatukee # 177
4025 E. Chandler Blvd., Ste. 38
Ahwatukee, AZ 85048
Phone: 480-759-2295

Glendale # 085
7720 West Bell Road
Glendale, AZ 85308
Phone: 623-776-7414

Mesa # 089
2050 East Baseline Rd.
Mesa, AZ 85204
Phone: 480-632-0951

Paradise Valley # 282
4726 E. Shea Blvd.
Phoenix, AZ 85028
Phone: 602-485-7788

**Phoenix
(Town & Country) # 090**
4821 N. 20th Street
Phoenix, AZ 85016
Phone: 602-912-9022

Scottsdale (North) # 087
7555 E. Frank Lloyd Wright
N. Scottsdale, AZ 85260
Phone: 480-367-8920

Scottsdale # 094
6202 N. Scottsdale Road
Scottsdale, AZ 85253
Phone: 480-948-9886

Surprise # 092
14095 West Grand Ave.
Surprise, AZ 85374
Phone: 623-546-1640

Tempe # 093
6460 S. McClintock Drive
Tempe, AZ 85283
Phone: 480-838-4142

**Tucson
(Crossroads) # 088**
4766 East Grant Road
Tucson, AZ 85712
Phone: 520-323-4500

**Tucson (Wilmot &
Speedway)# 095**
1101 N. Wilmot Rd.
Suite #147
Tucson, AZ 85712
Phone: 520-733-1313

**Tucson (Campbell & Limberlost)
191**
4209 N. Campbell Ave.
Tucson, AZ 85719
Phone: 520-325-0069

Tucson - Oro Valley # 096
7912 N. Oracle
Oro Valley, AZ 85704
Phone: 520-797-4207

CALIFORNIA

Agoura Hills
28941 Canwood Street
Agoura Hills, CA 91301
Phone: 818-865-8217

Alameda # 109
2217 South Shore Center
Alameda, CA 94501
Phone: 510-769-5450

Aliso Viejo # 195
The Commons
26541 Aliso Creek Road
Aliso Viejo, CA 92656
Phone: 949-643-5531

Arroyo Grande # 117
955 Rancho Parkway
Arroyo Grande, CA 93420
Phone: 805-474-6114

Bakersfield # 014
8200-C 21 Stockdale Hwy.
Bakersfield, CA 93311
Phone: 661-837-8863

Berkeley #186
1885 University Ave.
Berkeley, CA 94703
Phone: 510-204-9074

Bixby Knolls # 116
4121 Atlantic Ave.
Bixby Knolls, CA 90807
Phone: 562-988-0695

Brea # 011
2500 E. Imperial Hwy.
Suite 177
Brea, CA 92821
Phone 714-257-1180

Brentwood # 201
5451 Lone Tree Way
Brentwood, CA 94513
Phone: 925-516-3044

Burbank # 124
214 East Alameda
Burbank, CA 91502
Phone: 818-848-4299

Camarillo # 114
363 Carmen Drive
Camarillo, CA 93010
Phone: 805-388-1925

Campbell # 073
1875 Bascom Avenue
Campbell, CA 95008
Phone: 408-369-7823

Capitola # 064
3555 Clares Street #D
Capitola, CA 95010
Phone: 831-464-0115

Carlsbad # 220
2629 Gateway Road
Carlsbad, CA 92009
Phone: 760-603-8473

Castro Valley # 084
22224 Redwood Road
Castro Valley, CA 94546
Phone: 510-538-2738

Cathedral City # 118
67-720 East Palm Cyn.
Cathedral City, CA 92234
Phone: 760-202-0090

Cerritos # 104
12861 Towne Center Drive
Cerritos, CA 90703
Phone: 562-402-5148

Chatsworth # 184
10330 Mason Ave.
Chatsworth, CA 91311
Phone: 818-341-3010

Chico # 199
801 East Ave., Suite #110
Chico, CA 95926
Phone: 530-343-9920

Chino Hills # 216
13911 Peyton Dr.
Chino Hills, CA 91709
Phone: 909-627-1404

Chula Vista # 120
878 Eastlake Parkway,
Suite 810
Chula Vista, CA 91914
Phone: 619-656-5370

Claremont # 214
475 W. Foothill Blvd.
Claremont, CA 91711
Phone: 909-625-8784

Clovis # 180
1077 N. Willow, Suite 101
Clovis, CA 93611
Phone: 559-325-3120

**Concord (Oak Grove
& Treat) # 083**
785 Oak Grove Road
Concord, CA 94518
Phone: 925-521-1134

Concord (Airport) # 060
1150 Concord Ave.
Concord, CA 94520
Phone: 925-689-2990

Corona # 213
2790 Cabot Drive, Ste. 165
Corona, CA 92883
Phone: 951-603-0299

Costa Mesa # 035
640 W. 17th Street
Costa Mesa, CA 92627
Phone: 949-642-5134

Culver City # 036
9290 Culver Blvd.
Culver City, CA 90232
Phone: 310-202-1108

Daly City # 074
417 Westlake Center
Daly City, CA 94015
Phone: 650-755-3825

Danville # 065
85 Railroad Ave.
Danville, CA 94526
Phone: 925-838-5757

Davis
885 Russell Blvd.
Davis, CA 95616
Phone: 530-757-2693

Eagle Rock # 055
1566 Colorado Blvd.
Eagle Rock, CA 90041
Phone: 323-257-6422

El Cerrito # 108
225 El Cerrito Plaza
El Cerrito, CA 94530
Phone: 510-524-7609

Elk Grove # 190
9670 Bruceville Road
Elk Grove, CA 95757
Phone: 916-686-9980

Emeryville # 072
5700 Christie Avenue
Emeryville, CA 94608
Phone: 510-658-8091

Encinitas # 025
115 N. El Camino Real, Suite A
Encinitas, CA 92024
Phone: 760-634-2114

Encino # 056
17640 Burbank Blvd.
Encino, CA 91316
Phone: 818-990-7751

Escondido # 105
1885 So. Centre City
Pkwy., Unit "A"
Escondido, CA 92025
Phone: 760-233-4020

Fair Oaks # 071
5309 Sunrise Blvd.
Fair Oaks, CA 95628
Phone: 916-863-1744

Fairfield # 101
1350 Gateway Blvd.,
Suite A1-A7
Fairfield, CA 94533
Phone: 707-434-0144

Folsom # 172
850 East Bidwell
Folsom, CA 95630
Phone: 916-817-8820

Fremont # 077
39324 Argonaut Way
Fremont, CA 94538
Phone: 510-794-1386

Fresno # 008
5376 N. Blackstone
Fresno, CA 93710
Phone: 559-222-4348

Glendale # 053
130 N. Glendale Ave.
Glendale, CA 91206
Phone: 818-637-2990

Goleta # 110
5767 Calle Real
Goleta, CA 93117
Phone: 805-692-2234

Granada Hills # 044
11114 Balboa Blvd.
Granada Hills, CA 91344
Phone: 818-368-6461

Hollywood
1600 N. Vine Street
Los Angeles, CA 90028
Phone: 323-856-0689

Huntington Bch. # 047
18681-101 Main Street
Huntington Bch., CA 92648
Phone: 714-848-9640

Huntington Bch. # 241
21431 Brookhurst St.
Huntington Bch., CA 92646
Phone: 714-968-4070

Huntington Harbor # 244
Huntington Harbour Mall
16821 Algonquin St.
Huntington Bch., CA 92649
Phone: 714-846-7307

**Irvine (Walnut Village Center)
037**
14443 Culver Drive
Irvine, CA 92604
Phone: 949-857-8108

**Irvine (University
Center) # 111**
4225 Campus Dr.
Irvine, CA 92612
Phone: 949-509-6138

**Irvine (Irvine &
Sand Cyn) # 210**
6222 Irvine Blvd.
Irvine, CA 92620
Phone: 949-551-6402

La Cañada # 042
475 Foothill Blvd.
La Canada, CA 91011
Phone: 818-790-6373

La Crescenta # 052
3433 Foothill Blvd.
LaCrescenta, CA 91214
Phone: 818-249-3693

La Quinta # 189
46-400 Washington Street
La Quinta, CA 92253
Phone: 760-777-1553

Lafayette # 115
3649 Mt. Diablo Blvd.
Lafayette, CA 94549
Phone: 925-299-9344

Laguna Hills # 039
24321 Avenue De La Carlota
Laguna Hills, CA 92653
Phone: 949-586-8453

Laguna Niguel # 103
32351 Street of the Golden
Lantern
Laguna Niguel, CA 92677
Phone: 949-493-8599

La Jolla # 020
8657 Villa LaJolla
Drive #210
La Jolla, CA 92037
Phone: 858-546-8629

La Mesa # 024
5495 Grossmont Center Dr.
La Mesa, CA 91942
Phone: 619-466-0105

Larkspur # 235
2052 Redwood Hwy
Larkspur, CA 94921
Phone: 415-945-7955

Livermore # 208
1122-A East Stanley Blvd.
Livermore, CA 94550
Phone: 925-243-1947

Long Beach (PCH) # 043
6451 E. Pacific Coast Hwy.
Long Beach, CA 90803
Phone: 562-596-4388

**Long Beach
(Bellflower Blvd.) # 194**
2222 Bellflower Blvd.
Long Beach, CA 90815
Phone: 562-596-2514

Los Altos # 127
2310 Homestead Rd.
Los Altos, CA 94024
Phone: 408-245-1917

**Los Angeles
(Silver Lake) # 017**
2738 Hyperion Ave.
Los Angeles, CA 90027
Phone: 323-665-6774

Los Angeles # 031
263 S. La Brea
Los Angeles, CA 90036
Phone: 323-965-1989

Los Angeles (Sunset Strip) # 192
8000 Sunset Blvd.
Los Angeles, CA 90046
Phone: 323-822-7663

Los Gatos # 181
15466 Los Gatos Blvd.
Los Gatos, CA 95032
Phone 408-356-2324

Manhattan Beach # 034
1821 Manhattan
Beach. Blvd.
Manhattan Bch., CA 90266
Phone: 310-372-1274

Manhattan Beach # 196
1800 Rosecrans Blvd.
Manhattan Beach,
CA 90266
Phone: 310-725-9800

Menlo Park # 069
720 Menlo Avenue
Menlo Park, CA 94025
Phone: 650-323-2134

Millbrae # 170
765 Broadway
Millbrae, CA 94030
Phone: 650-259-9142

Mission Viejo # 126
25410 Marguerite Parkway
Mission Viejo, CA 92692
Phone: 949-581-5638

Modesto # 009
3250 Dale Road
Modesto, CA 95356
Phone: 209-491-0445

Monrovia # 112
604 W. Huntington Dr.
Monrovia, CA 91016
Phone: 626-358-8884

Monterey # 204
570 Munras Ave., Ste. 20
Monterey, CA 93940
Phone: 831-372-2010

Morgan Hill # 202
17035 Laurel Road
Morgan Hill, CA 95037
Phone: 408-778-6409

Mountain View # 081
590 Showers Dr.
Mountain View, CA 94040
Phone: 650-917-1013

Napa # 128
3654 Bel Aire Plaza
Napa, CA 94558
Phone: 707-256-0806

Newbury Park # 243
125 N. Reino Road
Newbury Park, CA
Phone: 805-375-1984

Newport Beach # 125
8086 East Coast Highway
Newport Beach, CA 92657
Phone: 949-494-7404

Novato # 198
7514 Redwood Blvd.
Novato, CA 94945
Phone: 415-898-9359

**Oakland
(Lakeshore) # 203**
3250 Lakeshore Ave.
Oakland, CA 94610
Phone: 510-238-9076

**Oakland
(Rockridge) # 231**
5727 College Ave.
Oakland, CA 94618
Phone: 510-923-9428

Oceanside # 22
2570 Vista Way
Oceanside, CA 92054
Phone: 760-433-9994

Orange # 046
2114 N. Tustin St.
Orange, CA 92865
Phone: 714-283-5697

Pacific Grove # 008
1170 Forest Avenue
Pacific Grove, CA 93950
Phone: 831-656-0180

Palm Desert # 003
44-250 Town Center Way, Suite C6
Palm Desert, CA 92260
Phone: 760-340-2291

Palmdale # 185
39507 10th Street West
Palmdale, CA 93551
Phone: 661-947-2890

Palo Alto # 207
855 El Camino Real
Palo Alto, CA 94301
Phone: 650-327-7018

**Pasadena
(S. Lake Ave.) # 179**
345 South Lake Ave.
Pasadena, CA 91101
Phone: 626-395-9553

**Pasadena
(S. Arroyo Pkwy.) # 051**
610 S. Arroyo Parkway
Pasadena, CA 91105
Phone: 626-568-9254

**Pasadena
(Hastings Ranch) # 171**
467 Rosemead Blvd.
Pasadena, CA 91107
Phone: 626-351-3399

Petaluma # 107
169 North McDowell Blvd.
Petaluma, CA 94954
Phone: 707-769-2782

Pinole # 230
2742 Pinole Valley Rd.
Pinole, CA 94564
Phone: 510-222-3501

Pleasanton # 066
4040 Pimlico #150
Pleasanton, CA 94588
Phone: 925-225-3600

Rancho Cucamonga # 217
6401 Haven Ave.
Rancho Cucamonga, CA 91737
Phone: 909-476-1410

**Rancho Palos Verdes
057**
28901 S. Western Ave. #243
Rancho Palos Verdes,
CA 90275
Phone: 310-832-1241

Rancho Palos Verdes # 233
31176 Hawthorne Blvd.
Rancho Palos Verdes, CA 90275
Phone: 310-544-1727

Rancho Santa Margarita # 027
30652 Santa Margarita Pkwy. Suite F102
Rancho Santa Margarita, CA 92688
Phone: 949-888-3640

Redding # 219
845 Browning St.
Redding, CA 96003
Phone: 530-223-4875

Redlands # 099
552 Orange Street Plaza
Redlands, CA 92374
Phone: 909-798-3888

Redondo Beach # 038
1761 S. Elena Avenue
Redondo Bch., CA 90277
Phone: 310-316-1745

Riverside # 15
6225 Riverside Plaza
Riverside, CA 92506
Phone: 951-682-4684

Roseville # 80
1117 Roseville Square
Roseville, CA 95678
Phone: 916-784-9084

Sacramento (Folsom Blvd.) # 175
5000 Folsom Blvd.
Sacramento, CA 95819
Phone: 916-456-1853

Sacramento (Fulton & Marconi) # 070
2625 Marconi Avenue
Sacramento, CA 95821
Phone: 916-481-8797

San Carlos # 174
1482 El Camino Real
San Carlos, CA 94070
Phone: 650-594-2138

San Clemente # 016
638 Camino DeLosMares, Sp.#115-G
San Clemente, CA 92673
Phone: 949-240-9996

San Diego (Hillcrest) # 026
1090 University Ste. G100-107
San Diego, CA 92103
Phone: 619-296-3122

San Diego (Point Loma) # 188
2401 Truxtun Rd., Ste. 300
San Diego, CA 92106
Phone: 619-758-9272

San Diego (Pacific Beach) # 021
1211 Garnet Avenue
San Diego, CA 92109
Phone: 858-272-7235

San Diego (Carmel Mtn. Ranch) # 023
11955 Carmel Mtn. Rd. #702
San Diego, CA 92128
Phone: 858-673-0526

San Diego (Scripps Ranch) # 221
9850 Hibert Street
San Diego, CA 92131
Phone: 858-549-9185

San Dimas # 028
856 Arrow Hwy. "C"
Target Center
San Dimas, CA 91773
Phone: 909-305-4757

San Francisco (9th Street) # 078
555 9th Street
San Francisco, CA 94103
Phone: 415-863-1292

San Francisco (Masonic Ave.) # 100
3 Masonic Avenue
San Francisco, CA 94118
Phone: 415-346-9964

San Francisco (North Beach) # 019
401 Bay Street
San Francisco, CA 94133
Phone: 415-351-1013

San Francisco (Stonestown) # 236
265 Winston Dr.
San Francisco, CA 94132
Phone: 415-665-1835

San Gabriel # 032
7260 N. Rosemead Blvd.
San Gabriel, CA 91775
Phone: 626-285-5862

San Jose (Bollinger) # 232
7250 Bollinger Rd.
San Jose, CA 95129
Phone: 408-873-7384

San Jose
(Coleman Ave) # 212
635 Coleman Ave.
San Jose, CA 95110
Phone: 408-298-9731

San Jose
(Old Almaden) # 063
5353 Almaden Expressway #J-38
San Jose, CA 95118
Phone: 408-927-9091

San Jose
(Westgate West) # 062
5269 Prospect
San Jose, CA 95129
Phone: 408-446-5055

San Luis Obispo # 041
3977 Higuera Street
San Luis Obispo, CA 93401
Phone: 805-783-2780

San Mateo
(Grant Street) # 067
1820-22 S. Grant Street
San Mateo, CA 94402
Phone: 650-570-6140

San Mateo
(Hillsdale) # 245
45 W Hillsdale Blvd
San Mateo, CA 94403
Phone: 650-286-1509

San Rafael # 061
337 Third Street
San Rafael, CA 94901
Phone: 415-454-9530

Santa Ana # 113
3329 South Bristol Street
Santa Ana, CA 92704
Phone: 714-424-9304

Santa Barbara
(S. Milpas St.) # 059
29 S. Milpas Street
Santa Barbara, CA 93103
Phone: 805-564-7878

Santa Barbara
(De La Vina) # 183
3025 De La Vina
Santa Barbara, CA 93105
Phone: 805-563-7383

Santa Cruz # 193
700 Front Street
Santa Cruz, CA 95060
Phone: 831-425-0140

Santa Maria # 239
1303 S. Bradley Road
Santa Maria, CA 93454
Phone: 805-925-1657

Santa Monica # 006
3212 Pico Blvd.
Santa Monica, CA 90405
Phone: 310-581-0253

Santa Rosa
(Cleveland Ave.) # 075
3225 Cleveland Avenue
Santa Rosa, CA 95403
Phone: 707-525-1406

Santa Rosa
(Santa Rosa Ave.) # 178
2100 Santa Rosa Ave.
Santa Rosa, CA 95407
Phone: 707-535-0788

Sherman Oaks # 049
14119 Riverside Drive
Sherman Oaks, CA 91423
Phone: 818-789-2771

Simi Valley # 030
2975-A Cochran St.
Simi Valley, CA 93065
Phone: 805-520-3135

South Pasadena # 018
613 Mission Street
South Pasadena, CA 91030
Phone: 626-441-6263

South San Francisco # 187
301 McLellan Dr.
So. San Francisco,
CA 94080
Phone: 650-583-6401

Stockton # 076
6535 Pacific Avenue
Stockton, CA 95207
Phone: 209-951-7597

Studio City # 122
11976 Ventura Blvd.
Studio City, CA 91604
Phone: 818-509-0168

Sunnyvale # 068
727 Sunnyvale/
Saratoga Rd.
Sunnyvale, CA 94087
Phone: 408-481-9082

Temecula # 102
40665 Winchester Rd., Bldg. B,
Ste. 4-6
Temecula, CA 92591
Phone: 951-296-9964

Templeton # 211
1111 Rossi Road
Templeton, CA 93465
Phone: 805-434-9562

Thousand Oaks # 196
451 Avenida
De Los Arboles
Thousand Oaks, CA 91360
Phone: 805-492-7107

Toluca Lake # 054
10130 Riverside Drive
Toluca Lake, CA 91602
Phone: 818-762-2787

Torrance
(Hawthorne Blvd.) # 121
19720 Hawthorne Blvd.
Torrance, CA 90503
Phone: 310-793-8585

Torrance (Rolling
Hills Plaza) # 029
2545 Pacific Coast Highway
Torrance, CA 90505
Phone: 310-326-9520

Tustin # 197
12932 Newport Avenue
Tustin, CA 92780
Phone: 714-669-3752

Upland # 010
333 So. Mountain Avenue
Upland, CA 91786
Phone: 909-946-4799

Valencia # 013
26517 Bouquet Canyon Rd
Santa Clarita, CA 91350
Phone: 661-263-3796

Ventura # 045
1795 S. Victoria Avenue
Ventura, CA 93003
Phone: 805-650-9977

Ventura – Midtown
103 S. Mills Road Suite 104
Ventura, CA 93003
Phone: 805-658-2664

Walnut Creek # 123
1372 So. California Blvd.
Walnut Creek, CA 94596
Phone: 925-945-1674

West Hills # 050
6751 Fallbrook Ave.
West Hills, CA 91307
Phone: 818-347-2591

West Hollywood # 040
7304 Santa Monica Blvd.
West Hollywood, CA 90046
Phone: 323-851-9772

West Hollywood # 173
8611 Santa Monica Blvd.
West Hollywood, CA 90069
Phone: 310-657-0152

West Los Angeles
(National Blvd.) # 007
10850 National Blvd.
West Los Angeles, CA 90064
Phone: 310-470-1917

West Los Angeles
S. Sepulveda Blvd.) # 119
3456 S. Sepulveda Blvd.
West Los Angeles,
CA 90034
Phone: 310-836-2458

West Los Angeles
(Olympic) # 215
11755 W. Olympic Blvd.
West Los Angeles,
CA 90064
Phone: 310-477-5949

Westchester # 033
8645 S. Sepulveda
Westchester, CA 90045
Phone: 310-338-9238

Westlake Village # 058
3835 E. Thousand
Oaks Blvd.
Westlake Village, CA 91362
Phone: 805-494-5040

Westwood # 234
1000 Glendon Avenue
Los Angeles, CA 90024
Phone: 310-824-1495

* Store does not carry alcohol

Whittier # 048
15025 E. Whittier Blvd.
Whittier, CA 90603
Phone: 562-698-1642

Woodland Hills # 209
21054 Clarendon St.
Woodland Hills, CA 91364
Phone: 818-712-9475

Yorba Linda # 176
19655 Yorba Linda Blvd.
Yorba Linda, CA 92886
Phone: 714-970-0116

CONNECTICUT
Danbury # 525
113 Mill Plain Rd.
Danbury, CT 06811
Phone: 203-739-0098
Alcohol: Beer Only

Darien # 522
436 Boston Post Rd.
Darien, CT 06820
Phone: 203-656-1414
Alcohol: Beer Only

Fairfield # 523
2258 Black Rock Turnpike
Fairfield, CT 06825
Phone: 203-330-8301
Alcohol: Beer Only

Orange # 524
560 Boston Post Road
Orange, CT 06477
Phone: 203-795-5505
Alcohol: Beer Only

West Hartford # 526
1489 New Britain Ave.
West Hartford, CT 06110
Phone: 860-561-4771
Alcohol: Beer Only

Westport # 521
400 Post Road East
Westport, CT 06880
Phone: 203-226-8966
Alcohol: Beer Only

DELAWARE
Wilmington* # 536
5605 Concord Pike
Wilmington, DE 19803
Phone: 302-478-8494

DISTRICT OF COLUMBIA
Washington # 653
1101 25th Street NW
Washington, DC 20037
Phone: 202-296-1921

GEORGIA
Athens
1850 Epps Bridge Parkway
Athens, GA 30606
Phone: 706-583-8934

**Atlanta
(Buckhead) # 735**
3183 Peachtree Rd NE
Atlanta, GA 30305
Phone: 404-842-0907

Atlanta (Midtown) # 730
931 Monroe Dr., NE
Atlanta, GA 30308
Phone: 404-815-9210

Marietta # 732
4250 Roswell Road
Marietta, GA 30062
Phone: 678-560-3585

Norcross # 734
5185 Peachtree Parkway, Bld. 1200
Norcross, GA 30092
Phone: 678-966-9236

Roswell # 733
635 W. Crossville Road
Roswell, GA 30075
Phone: 770-645-8505

Sandy Springs # 731
6277 Roswell Road NE
Sandy Springs, GA 30328
Phone: 404-236-2414

ILLINOIS
Algonquin # 699
1800 South Randall Road
Algonquin, IL 60102
Phone: 847-854-4886

Arlington Heights # 687
17 W. Rand Road
Arlington Heights, IL 60004
Phone: 847-506-0752

Batavia # 689
1942 West Fabyan
Parkway #222
Batavia, IL 60510
Phone: 630-879-3234

* Store does not carry alcohol

**Chicago
River North) # 696**
44 E. Ontario St.
Chicago, IL 60611
Phone: 312-951-6369

**Chicago
(Lincoln & Grace) # 688**
3745 North Lincoln Avenue
Chicago, IL 60613
Phone: 773-248-4920

**Chicago
(Lincoln Park) # 691**
1840 North Clybourn
Avenue #200
Chicago, IL 60614
Phone: 312-274-9733

*Chicago (South Loop) – coming
soon!*
1147 S. Wabash Ave.
Chicago, IL 60605
Phone: TBD

*Chicago (Lakeview) – coming
soon!*
667 W. Diversey Pkwy
Chicago, IL 60614
Phone: 773-935-7255

Downers Grove # 683
122 Ogden Ave.
Downers Grove, IL 60515
Phone: 630-241-1662

Glen Ellyn # 680
680 Roosevelt Rd.
Glen Ellyn, IL 60137
Phone: 630-858-5077

Glenview # 681
1407 Waukegan Road
Glenview, IL 60025
Phone: 847-657-7821

La Grange # 685
25 North La Grange Road
La Grange, IL 60525
Phone: 708-579-0838

Lake Zurich # 684
735 W. Route 22**
Lake Zurich, IL 60047
Phone: 847-550-7827
[**For accurate driving directions
using GPS, please use
735 W Main Street]

Naperville # 690
44 West Gartner Road
Naperville, IL 60540
Phone: 630-355-4389

Northbrook # 682
127 Skokie Blvd.
Northbrook, IL 60062
Phone: 847-498-9076

Oak Park # 697
483 N. Harlem Ave.
Oak Park, IL 60301
Phone: 708-386-1169

Orland Park # 686
14924 S. La Grange Road
Orland Park, IL 60462
Phone: 708-349-9021

Park Ridge # 698
190 North Northwest Highway
Park Ridge, IL 60068
Phone: 847-292-1108

INDIANA
**Indianapolis
(Castleton) # 671**
5473 East 82nd Street
Indianapolis, IN 46250
Phone: 317-595-8950

**Indianapolis
(West 86th) # 670**
2902 West 86th Street
Indianapolis, IN 46268
Phone: 317-337-1880

IOWA
West Des Moines
6305 Mills Civic Parkway
West Des Moines, IA 50266
Phone: 515-225-3820

KANSAS – Coming soon!
Leawood – coming soon!
4201 W 119th Street
Leawood, KS 66209
Phone: TBD

MAINE
Portland
87 Marginal Way
Portland, ME 04101
Phone: 207-699-3799

* Store does not carry alcohol

MARYLAND

Annapolis* # 650
160 F Jennifer Road
Annapolis, MD 21401
Phone: 410-573-0505

Bethesda* # 645
6831 Wisconsin Avenue
Bethesda, MD 20815
Phone: 301-907-0982

Columbia* # 658
6610 Marie Curie Dr. (Int. of 175
& 108)
Elkridge, MD 21075
Phone: 410-953-8139

Gaithersburg* # 648
18270 Contour Rd.
Gaithersburg, MD 20877
Phone: 301-947-5953

Pikesville* # 655
1809 Reisterstown Road, Suite
#121
Pikesville, MD 21208
Phone: 410-484-8373

Rockville* # 642
12268-H Rockville Pike
Rockville, MD 20852
Phone: 301-468-6656

Silver Spring* # 652
10741 Columbia Pike
Silver Spring, MD 20901
Phone: 301-681-1675

Towson* # 649
1 E. Joppa Rd.
Towson, MD 21286
Phone: 410-296-9851

MASSACHUSETTS

Acton* # 511
145 Great Road
Acton, MA 01720
Phone: 978-266-8908

Arlington* # 505
1427 Massachusetts Ave.
Arlington, MA 02476
Phone: 781-646-9138

Boston #510
899 Boylston Street
Boston, MA 02115
Phone: 617-262-6505

Brookline # 501
1317 Beacon Street
Brookline, MA 02446
Phone: 617-278-9997

Burlington* # 515
51 Middlesex Turnpike
Burlington, MA 01803
Phone: 781-273-2310

Cambridge
748 Memorial Drive
Cambridge, MA 02139
Phone: 617-491-8582

**Cambridge
(Fresh Pond)* # 517**
211 Alewife Brook Pkwy
Cambridge, MA 02138
Phone: 617-498-3201

Framingham # 503
659 Worcester Road
Framingham, MA 01701
Phone: 508-935-2931

Hadley* # 512
375 Russell Street
Hadley, MA 01035
Phone: 413-587-3260

Hanover* # 513
1775 Washington Street
Hanover, MA 02339
Phone: 781-826-5389

Hyannis* # 514
Christmas Tree Promenade
655 Route 132, Unit 4-A
Hyannis, MA 02601
Phone: 508-790-3008

Needham Hts* 504
958 Highland Avenue
Needham Hts, MA 02494
Phone: 781-449-6993

Peabody* # 516
300 Andover Street,
Suite 15
Peabody, MA 01960
Phone: 978-977-5316

Saugus* # 506
358 Broadway, Unit B
(Shops @ Saugus, Rte. 1)
Saugus, MA 01906
Phone: 781-231-0369

* Store does not carry alcohol

Shrewsbury* # 508
77 Boston Turnpike
Shrewsbury, MA 01545
Phone: 508-755-9560

Tyngsboro* # 507
440 Middlesex Road
Tyngsboro, MA 01879
Phone: 978-649-2726

West Newton* # 509
1121 Washington St.
West Newton, MA 02465
Phone: 617-244-1620

MICHIGAN
Ann Arbor # 678
2398 East Stadium Blvd.
Ann Arbor, MI 48104
Phone: 734-975-2455

Farmington Hills # 675
31221 West 14 Mile Road
Farmington Hills, MI 48334
Phone: 248-737-4609

Grosse Pointe # 665
17028 Kercheval Ave.
Grosse Pointe, MI 48230
Phone: 313-640-7794

Northville # 667
20490 Haggerty Road
Northville, MI 48167
Phone: 734-464-3675

Rochester Hills # 668
3044 Walton Blvd.
Rochester Hills, MI 48309
Phone: 248-375-2190

Royal Oak # 674
27880 Woodward Ave.
Royal Oak, MI 48067
Phone: 248-582-9002

MINNESOTA
Maple Grove # 713
12105 Elm Creek Blvd. N.
Maple Grove, MN 55369
Phone: 763-315-1739

Minnetonka # 714
11220 Wayzata Blvd
Minnetonka, MN 55305
Phone: 952-417-9080

Rochester
1200 16th St. SW
Rochester, NY 55902
Phone: 952-417-9080

St. Louis Park # 710
4500 Excelsior Blvd.
St. Louis Park, MN 55416
Phone: 952-285-1053

St. Paul # 716
484 Lexington Parkway S.
St. Paul, MN 55116
Phone: 651-698-3119

Woodbury # 715
8960 Hudson Road
Woodbury, MN 55125
Phone: 651-735-0269

MISSOURI
Brentwood # 792
48 Brentwood
Promenade Court
Brentwood, MO 63144
Phone: 314-963-0253

Chesterfield # 693
1679 Clarkson Road
Chesterfield, MO 63017
Phone: 636-536-7846

Creve Coeur # 694
11505 Olive Blvd.
Creve Coeur, MO 63141
Phone: 314-569-0427

Des Peres # 695
13343 Manchester Rd.
Des Peres, MO 63131
Phone: 314-984-5051

***Kansas City –
coming soon!***
8600 Ward Parkway
Kansas City, MO 64114
Phone: TBD

NEBRASKA
Lincoln
3120 Pine Lake Road,
Suite R
Lincoln, NE 68516
Phone: 402-328-0120

Omaha # 714
10305 Pacific St.
Omaha, NE 68114
Phone: 402-391-3698

* Store does not carry alcohol

NEVADA

Anthem # 280
10345 South Eastern Ave.
Henderson, NV 89052
Phone: 702-407-8673

Carson City # 281
3790 US Highway 395 S, Suite 401
Carson City, NV 89705
Phone: 775-267-2486

Henderson # 097
2716 North Green Valley Parkway
Henderson, NV 89014
Phone: 702-433-6773

**Las Vegas
(Decatur Blvd.) # 098**
2101 S. Decatur Blvd.,
Suite 25
Las Vegas, NV 89102
Phone: 702-367-0227

**Las Vegas
(Summerlin) # 086**
7575 West Washington, Suite 117
Las Vegas, NV 89128
Phone: 702-242-8240

Reno # 082
5035 S. McCarran Blvd.
Reno, NV 89502
Phone: 775-826-1621

NEW JERSEY

Edgewater* # 606
715 River Road
Edgewater, NJ 07020
Phone: 201-945-5932

Florham Park* # 604
186 Columbia Turnpike
Florham Park, NJ 07932
Phone: 973-514-1511

Marlton* # 631
300 P Route 73 South
Marlton, NJ 08053
Phone: 856-988-3323

Millburn* # 609
187 Millburn Ave.
Millburn, NJ 07041
Phone: 973-218-0912

Paramus* # 605
404 Rt. 17 North
Paramus, NJ 07652
Phone: 201-265-9624

Princeton # 607
3528 US 1
(Brunswick Pike)
Princeton, NJ 08540
Phone: 609-897-0581

Shrewsbury*
1031 Broad St.
Shrewsbury, NJ 07702
Phone: 732-389-2535

Wayne* # 632
1172 Hamburg Turnpike
Wayne, NJ 07470
Phone: 973-692-0050

Westfield # 601
155 Elm St.
Westfield, NJ 07090
Phone: 908-301-0910

Westwood* # 602
20 Irvington Street
Westwood, NJ 07675
Phone: 201-263-0134

NEW MEXICO

Albuquerque # 166
8928 Holly Ave. NE
Albuquerque, NM 87122
Phone: 505-796-0311

**Albuquerque
(Uptown) # 167**
2200 Uptown Loop NE
Albuquerque, NM 87110
Phone: 505-883-3662

Santa Fe # 165
530 W. Cordova Road
Santa Fe, NM 87505
Phone: 505-995-8145

NEW YORK

Brooklyn # 558
130 Court St
Brooklyn, NY 11201
Phone: 718-246-8460
Alcohol: Beer Only

Commack # 551
5010 Jericho Turnpike
Commack, NY 11725
Phone: 631-493-9210
Alcohol: Beer Only

* Store does not carry alcohol

Hartsdale # 533
215 North Central Avenue
Hartsdale, NY 10530
Phone: 914-997-1960
Alcohol: Beer Only

Hewlett # 554
1280 West Broadway
Hewlett, NY 11557
Phone: 516-569-7191
Alcohol: Beer Only

Lake Grove # 556
137 Alexander Ave.
Lake Grove, NY 11755
Phone: 631-863-2477
Alcohol: Beer Only

Larchmont # 532
1260 Boston Post Road
Larchmont, NY 10538
Phone: 914-833-9110
Alcohol: Beer Only

Merrick # 553
1714 Merrick Road
Merrick, NY 11566
Phone: 516-771-1012
Alcohol: Beer Only

**New York
(72nd & Broadway) # 542**
2075 Broadway
New York, NY 10023
Phone: 212-799-0028
Alcohol: Beer Only

**New York
(Chelsea) # 543**
675 6th Ave
New York, NY 10010
Phone: 212-255-2106
Alcohol: Beer Only

New York (Union Square Grocery) # 540
142 E. 14th St.
New York, NY 10003
Phone: 212-529-4612
Alcohol: Beer Only

New York (Union Square Wine) # 541
138 E. 14th St.
New York, NY 10003
Phone: 212-529-6326
Alcohol: Wine Only

Oceanside # 552
3418 Long Beach Rd.
Oceanside, NY 11572
Phone: 516-536-9163
Alcohol: Beer Only

Plainview # 555
425 S. Oyster Bay Rd.
Plainview, NY 11803
Phone: 516-933-6900
Alcohol: Beer Only

Queens # 557
90-30 Metropolitan Ave.
Queens, NY 11374
Phone: 718-275-1791
Alcohol: Beer Only

Scarsdale # 531
727 White Plains Rd.
Scarsdale, NY 10583
Phone: 914-472-2988
Alcohol: Beer Only

***Staten Island
– coming soon!***
2385 Richmond Ave
Staten Island, NY 10314
Phone: TBD
Alcohol: Beer Only

NORTH CAROLINA

Cary # 741
1393 Kildaire Farms Rd.
Cary, NC 27511
Phone: 919-465-5984

Chapel Hill # 745
1800 E. Franklin St.
Chapel Hill, NC 27514
Phone: 919-918-7871

**Charlotte
(Midtown) # 744**
1133 Metropolitan Ave., Ste. 100
Charlotte, NC 28204
Phone: 704-334-0737

Charlotte (North) # 743
1820 East Arbors Dr.** (corner of
W. Mallard Creek Church Rd. &
Senator Royall Dr.)
Charlotte, NC 28262
Phone: 704-688-9578
[**For accurate driving directions
on the web, please use 1820
W. Mallard Creek Church Rd.]

* Store does not carry alcohol

Charlotte (South) # 742
6418 Rea Rd.
Charlotte, NC 28277
Phone: 704-543-5249

Raleigh # 746
3000 Wake Forest Rd.
Raleigh, NC 27609
Phone: 919-981-7422

OHIO

Cincinnati # 669
7788 Montgomery Road
Cincinnati, OH 45236
Phone: 513-984-3452

Columbus # 679
3888 Townsfair Way
Columbus, OH 43219
Phone: 614-473-0794

Dublin # 672
6355 Sawmill Road
Dublin, OH 43017
Phone: 614-793-8505

Kettering # 673
328 East Stroop Road
Kettering, OH 45429
Phone: 937-294-5411

Westlake # 677
175 Market Street
Westlake, OH 44145
Phone: 440-250-1592

Woodmere # 676
28809 Chagrin Blvd.
Woodmere, OH 44122
Phone: 216-360-9320

OREGON

Beaverton # 141
11753 S. W. Beaverton
Hillsdale Hwy.
Beaverton, OR 97005
Phone: 503-626-3794

Bend # 150
63455 North
Highway 97, Ste. 4
Bend, OR 97701
Phone: 541-312-4198

Clackamas # 152
9345 SE 82nd Ave (across from
Home Depot)
Happy Valley, OR 97086
Phone: 503-771-6300

Corvallis # 154
1550 NW 9th Street
Corvallis, OR 97330
Phone: 541-753-0048

Eugene # 145
85 Oakway Center
Eugene, OR 97401
Phone: 541-485-1744

Hillsboro # 149
2285 NW 185th Ave.
Hillsboro, OR 97124
Phone: 503-645-8321

Lake Oswego # 142
15391 S. W. Bangy Rd.
Lake Oswego, OR 97035
Phone: 503-639-3238

Portland (SE) # 143
4715 S. E. 39th Avenue
Portland, OR 97202
Phone: 503-777-1601

Portland (NW) # 146
2122 N.W. Glisan
Portland, OR 97210
Phone: 971-544-0788

**Portland
(Hollywood) # 144**
4121 N.E. Halsey St.
Portland, OR 97213
Phone: 503-284-1694

Salem – coming soon!
4450 Commercial St.,
Suite 100
Salem, OR 97302
Phone: TBD

PENNSYLVANIA

Ardmore* # 635
112 Coulter Avenue
Ardmore, PA 19003
Phone: 610-658-0645

Jenkintown* # 633
933 Old York Road
Jenkintown, PA 19046
Phone: 215-885-524

Media* # 637
12 East State Street
Media, PA 19063
Phone: 610-891-2752

North Wales* # 639
1430 Bethlehem Pike
(corner SR 309 & SR 63)
North Wales, PA 19454
Phone: 215-646-5870

Philadelphia* # 634
2121 Market Street
Philadelphia, PA 19103
Phone: 215-569-9282

Pittsburgh* # 638
6343 Penn Ave.
Pittsburgh, PA 15206
Phone: 412-363-5748

Pittsburgh*
- coming soon!
1600 Washington Road
Pittsburgh, PA 15228
Phone: TBD

Wayne* # 632
171 East Swedesford Rd.
Wayne, PA 19087
Phone: 610-225-0925

RHODE ISLAND
Warwick* # 518
1000 Bald Hill Rd
Warwick, RI 02886
Phone: 401-821-5368

SOUTH CAROLINA
Greenville
59 Woodruff
Industrial Lane
Greenville, SC 29607
Phone: 864-286-0231

Mt. Pleasant –
coming soon!
401 Johnnie Dodds Blvd.
Mt. Pleasant, SC 29464
Phone: TBD

TENNESSEE
Nashville # 664
3909 Hillsboro Pike
Nashville, TN 37215
Phone: 615-297-6560
Alcohol: Beer Only

VIRGINIA
Alexandria # 647
612 N. Saint Asaph Street
Alexandria, VA 22314
Phone: 703-548-0611

Bailey's Crossroads # 644
5847 Leesburg Pike
Bailey's Crossroads,
VA 22041
Phone: 703-379-5883

Centreville # 654
14100 Lee Highway
Centreville, VA 20120
Phone: 703-815-0697

Fairfax # 643
9464 Main Street
Fairfax, VA 22031
Phone: 703-764-8550

Falls Church # 641
7514 Leesburg Turnpike
Falls Church, VA 22043
Phone: 703-288-0566

Newport News # 656
12551 Jefferson Ave.,
Suite #179
Newport News, VA 23602
Phone: 757-890-0235

Reston # 646
11958 Killingsworth Ave.
Reston, VA 20194
Phone: 703-689-0865

**Richmond
(Short Pump) # 659**
11331 W Broad St, Ste 161
Glen Allen, VA 23060
Phone: 804-360-4098

Springfield # 651
6394 Springfield Plaza
Springfield, VA 22150
Phone: 703-569-9301

Virginia Beach # 660
503 Hilltop Plaza
Virginia Beach, VA 23454
Phone: 757-422-4840

Williamsburg # 657
5000 Settlers Market Blvd
(corner of Monticello and
Settlers Market)**
Williamsburg, VA 23188
Phone: 757-259-2135
[**For accurate driving directions on the web, please use 5224
Monticello Ave.]

WASHINGTON

Ballard # 147
4609 14th Avenue NW
Seattle, WA 98107
Phone: 206-783-0498

Bellevue # 131
15400 N. E. 20th Street
Bellevue, WA 98007
Phone: 425-643-6885

Bellingham # 151
2410 James Street
Bellingham, WA 98225
Phone: 360-734-5166

Burien # 133
15868 1st. Avenue South
Burien, WA 98148
Phone: 206-901-9339

Everett # 139
811 S.E. Everett Mall Way
Everett, WA 98208
Phone: 425-513-2210

Federal Way # 134
1758 S. 320th Street
Federal Way, WA 98003
Phone: 253-529-9242

Issaquah # 138
1495 11th Ave. N.W.
Issaquah, WA 98027
Phone: 425-837-8088

Kirkland # 132
12632 120th Avenue N. E.
Kirkland, WA 98034
Phone: 425-823-1685

Lynnwood # 129
19500 Highway 99,
Suite 100
Lynnwood, WA 98036
Phone: 425-744-1346

Olympia # 156
Olympia West Center
1530 Black Lake Blvd.
Olympia, WA 98502
Phone: 360-352-7440

Redmond # 140
15932 Redmond Way
Redmond, WA 98052
Phone: 425-883-1624

Seattle (U. District) # 137
4555 Roosevelt Way NE
Seattle, WA 98105
Phone: 206-547-6299

**Seattle
(Queen Anne Hill) # 135**
112 West Galer St.
Seattle, WA 98119
Phone: 206-378-5536

**Seattle
(Capitol Hill) # 130**
1700 Madison St.
Seattle, WA 98122
Phone: 206-322-7268

Spokane – coming soon!
2975 East 29th Avenue
Spokane, WA 99223
Phone: TBD

University Place # 148
3800 Bridgeport Way West
University Place, WA 98466
Phone: 253-460-2672

Vancouver # 136
305 SE Chkalov Drive #B1
Vancouver, WA 98683
Phone: 360-883-9000

WISCONSIN

Glendale # 711
5600 North Port
Washington Road
Glendale, WI 53217
Phone: 414-962-3382

Madison # 712
1810 Monroe Street
Madison, WI 53711
Phone: 608-257-1916

Other titles in this cookbook series:

Cooking with All Things Trader Joe's
by **Deana Gunn & Wona Miniati**
ISBN 978-0-9799384-8-1

Cooking with Trader Joe's: Dinner's Done!
by **Deana Gunn & Wona Miniati**
ISBN 978-0-9799384-3-6

Cooking with Trader Joe's: Pack A Lunch!
by **Céline Cossou-Bordes**
ISBN 978-0-9799384-5-0

Cooking with Trader Joe's: Skinny Dish!
by **Jennifer K. Reilly, RD**
ISBN 978-0-9799384-7-4

Cooking with Trader Joe's: Lighten Up!
by **Susan Greeley, MS, RD**
ISBN 978-0-9799384-6-7

**Available everywhere books are sold.
Please visit us at**

CookTJ.com

Photo Credits

All photos of recipes on pages 10, 13, 14, 20, 22, 25, 26, 30, 33, 34, 37, 39, 40, 45, 46, 49, 52, 55, 59, 63, 65, 67, 69, 73, 77, 80, 81, 85, 86, 87, 89, 93, 97, 100, 101, 103, 105, 106, 108, 109, 111, 119, 122, 123, 124, 127, 129, 130, 135, 139, 140, 143, 145, 147, 148, 152, 153, 155, 156
© **Deana Gunn/Wona Miniati**

By **shutterstock.com**, background on cover, back cover and pages 9, 19, 37, 99, 121, 151, 163, 175 © javarman / Cover shopping bag © Ivonne Wierink / back cover top bowl, faded © Colorlife / spoon & fork © marinamik / photos of fruits, vegetables, line art etc. on pages: 79, 91, 99, 151 © Eric Gevaert / 44, 76, 79, 96, 115 © Iakov Kalinin / 15, 76, 96, 125, 131, 150, 155 © Jovan Nikolic / 1, 3, 9, 16, 19, 99, 121, 151, 163, 175 © javarman / 3, 9, 16, 18, 99, 107, 112, 121, 134, 151, 158, 160, 175 © Colorlife / 7, 51, 99, 151, 167, 175 © marinamik / 19, 34, 37, 38, 58, 96, 98, 166 © Nihongo / 3, 9, 35, 91, 99, 102 © Nikiparonak / 5, 121, 151 © Skyline / 8, 9, 19, 23, 29, 34, 53, 56, 61, 68, 82, 88, 99, 102, 111, 113, 115, 119, 120, 141, 151 © Elena Schweitzer / 9, 43, 53, 92, 120, 121, 125, 133, 150, 155, 158, 161 © Andrjuss / 16 © Fedorov Oleksiy / 17 © picturepartners / 38 © gcpics / 41, 54 © baldyrgan / 48 © Subbotina Anna / 49 © Elena Elisseeva / 49 © gresei / 57 © saiko3p / 59 © B.G. Smith / 84 © Angel Simon / 90 © agorulko / 84 © Chris Christou / 110 © niderlander / 115 © hvoya / 117 © Sally Scott / 117, 131, 132 © Madlen / 123 © Africa Studio / 128 © Yasonya / 134 © Olga Kadroff / 134 © infografick / 136 © Evgeny Karandaev / 148 © Viktar Malyshchyts / 165 © Alexkava / 168, 171, 172 © Nihongo / 175 © Stephen Coburn

By **Clipart ETC** © 2011 University of South Florida, illustrations on pages: 54, 61, 63, 67, 113

All other llustrations used by permission © **Dover Publications, Inc.** on pages: back cover, cover, 7, 19, 37, 43, 72, 75, 84, 88, 120, 121, 144, 150, 155, 159, 161, 163

Cooking with Trader Joe's cookbook Companion